# THE SMART
# SOLUTION BOOK

David Cotton

# THE SMART SOLUTION BOOK

## 68 TOOLS FOR BRAINSTORMING, PROBLEM SOLVING AND DECISION MAKING

**PEARSON**

Harlow, England • London • New York • Boston • San Francisco • Toronto • Sydney
Auckland • Singapore • Hong Kong • Tokyo • Seoul • Taipei • New Delhi
Cape Town • São Paulo • Mexico City • Madrid • Amsterdam • Munich • Paris • Milan

**PEARSON EDUCATION LIMITED**

Edinburgh Gate
Harlow CM20 2JE
United Kingdom
Tel: +44 (0)1279 623623
Web: www.pearson.com/uk

First published 2016 (print and electronic)

ISBN: 978-1-292-14231-9 (print)
    978-1-292-14236-4 (PDF)
    978-1-292-14232-6 (ePub)

**British Library Cataloguing-in-Publication Data**
A catalogue record for the print edition is available from the British Library

**Library of Congress Cataloging-in-Publication Data**
A catalog record for the print edition is available from the Library of Congress

10 9 8 7 6 5 4 3 2 1
19 18 17 16

Text design by Design Deluxe Ltd
Cover design by Two Associates

Print edition typeset in Helvetica Neue LT Pro 9.5pt by SPi Global
Printed by Ashford Colour Press Ltd, Gosport

NOTE THAT ANY PAGE CROSS REFERENCES REFER TO THE PRINT EDITION

# CONTENTS

## PART 4 LARGE GROUP PROBLEM-SOLVING TECHNIQUES 131

# PART 5 PROBLEM-SOLVING BUSINESS GAMES 145

# PART 6 SHARING AND IMPLEMENTING SOLUTIONS 165

# ABOUT THE AUTHOR

David Cotton spent 21 years with Arthur Andersen and PricewaterhouseCoopers (PwC) before becoming a freelance trainer in 2002. He has worked in 4 continents and more than 40 countries, delivering a wide range of training in management, leadership, communication skills, business networking, confidence building, dealing with difficult people, change management, business strategy, coaching and mentoring.

David's clients span local and national government and nearly every industry sector and include the European Parliament, European Commission and many of its agencies, the United Nations, BBC, Syrian Ministry for Foreign Affairs, Russian Federal Commission, Croatian MOD, PwC, most of the major Middle Eastern oil and gas companies, Manchester Business School and many others.

He is a Fellow of the British Institute for Learning and Development, a Member of the Institute of Leadership and Management and also has Diplomas in Training and Development, Hypnotherapy and NLP.

He has published scores of articles and more than a dozen books, including *Key Management Development Models* published by FT Publishing in 2015.

In his spare time, David is a regular columnist for a specialist music magazine and an avid collector of musical instruments. He has published more than 800 pieces of music and performs regularly with his band. He plays Association Croquet for his local club and, with his wife, appallingly bad golf.

Love and thanks to Jane, Philippa and Victoria Cotton.

# INTRODUCTION

I rather like solving problems. The most brilliant boss I ever had schooled me in this early in my career. 'I don't pay you to bring me problems,' he said, 'I pay you to find solutions. Come back when you have.' For a young professional, this was a great message. Most of my subsequent bosses responded far better to a request to choose the best solution than to solve a problem.

*The Smart Solution Book* is a collection of tools, techniques, ideas and ways of thinking about problem solving and decision making that synthesises ideas from a variety of sources – from traditional problem solving, through creativity to mass-scale collaborative approaches.

Many of the techniques outlined in the book can be scaled up or down in terms of the numbers involved in using them: from a one-person effort to a cast of thousands. Some are subtle variants of each other and some of them include their own variants. The trick for you, as a user, is to take a technique that looks relevant to your problem and then adapt it to work for you. Nothing here is set in stone – there is no single way of doing anything – and you can combine techniques to create something even more powerful.

Some years ago, I had the good fortune to attend a training course run by the European Commission entitled 'The Art of Participatory Leadership' (AOPL). It was based in large part on 'The Art of Hosting', a new approach to harnessing collective wisdom, regardless of the size of group involved in, say, problem solving or decision making. The essence of it was that well-structured collaborative thinking can yield far better results than a reliance on a small group of nominal leaders, that there is real power in the collective. In many organisations, the most senior people attempt to solve organisational problems almost independently of those who will be affected by the outcome. AOPL opened my eyes to a number of techniques that can be used by large groups of people working collaboratively to solve problems and make decisions that really matter to them and to those they serve.

There is a deep satisfaction in solving a problem, and collaborative problem solving creates an energy of its own. Many organisations list *teamwork* high on their list of values and expected competencies. When people work together towards a common goal, it creates a buzz – a real excitement – which brings people together and creates a bond and team spirit that generates many other spin-off benefits for the organisation. Personal agendas are set to one side and people start to realise that, collectively, they can achieve far more than through their individual or corporate silos.

Most of the collaborative problems solving techniques detailed here deny the dominant, aggressive or senior people a louder voice – everyone has an equal say and the quieter people are given a voice that they may lack in day-to-day work. The broader spread of ideas yields more creative and thoughtful solutions which work for a greater number of people. It can take a certain courage, in a senior position, to relinquish some of your assumed authority and allow more junior people a voice. Also, it will vastly increase the respect that others have for you as a leader. The days of command and control leadership are, largely, gone. Those who still embrace it will find themselves increasingly isolated from their workforces. The new generation – the *Millennials* – do not respect people simply because they have a title and a higher pay grade, but expect to see their bosses do something to earn respect. They have grown up in a society in which the gap between them and their parents, and them and their teachers, has narrowed and the voice of authority is as likely to be laughed at as to be entertained seriously. The new generation has seen more of the world and, often, has a greater social conscience than its forebears had at the same age. The older generation is often intent on cloning younger people in its own image. The younger people are unlikely to stay in an organisation long enough to be cloned. Indeed, they are likely to change professions regularly throughout their working life. Recently, I ran a workshop for a large professional organisation. The participants were of mixed grades from newly appointed assistants to senior partners. A partner declared that everyone in the room had the single goal of becoming a partner in the organisation. I suggested that most would not stay long enough to become partners, nor had any ambition of doing so. The senior partner asked for a show of hands. Of the 30 or so people in the room, only two declared their intention to reach partnership level.

The Millennials want to be a part of the decision-making process, regardless of their level of experience, and many of the techniques described here allow them that voice. It does not matter that they lack the experience of more senior people. Their fresh perspective and optimism may bring a different texture to otherwise staid decision-making and problem-solving processes. Old timers may find reasons why something cannot be done. Younger people may bring sufficient enthusiasm to find ways of making it happen.

This book offers ways of engaging people at all levels to solve problems, often in fun, dynamic and unexpected ways. For good measure, I have thrown in some more traditional problem-solving methods, too.

Throughout the book, I talk about, 'business,' problems, used as a blanket term for any kind of organisational problem. Whether you work in the private sector, public sector, charity, social enterprise or voluntary organisation, the methods described here can work as they are or can be made to fit with very little tailoring. If an example of how to use a technique appears to be based in a different sector than your own, you will find you can adapt it very easily to fit your situation.

Throughout the book, too, I talk about *brainstorming*. At its simplest level, brainstorming is just calling out and noting ideas without discussing them until no more ideas are forthcoming. Standard, traditional brainstorming on its own is not terribly effective, for reasons that become clear when you read about *brain-friendly brainstorming* later, but the basic premise of brainstorming is a building block in many of the techniques documented here.

I refer to those helping to solve a problem as *participants*. You will find guidance on how to prepare them to be useful participants!

As you read about each tool, model or idea, you will find sufficient information to know how you can use that tool in practice, where you can find more information about it (where that exists) and, in many cases, start to apply it immediately in your own working life. Some of the methods are my own inventions, and this is the only place in which you will find them documented.

This book will help you to:

■ frame problems so that they can be solved (and so help in the decision-making process);

■ find (often multiple) solutions to the most intractable problems;

■ enjoy the process of problem solving, whether alone or in collaboration with others;

■ become more creative in your thinking so that, over time, solutions begin to present themselves;

■ make decisions with more confidence, knowing that you have explored every avenue before committing to those decisions.

To get the best out of the book:

1   Read the introductory sections on barriers to problem solving, framing a problem and stages in problem solving.

2   Determine whether you will attempt to solve the problem alone, with a small group of people or with a large group.

3   Use Part 1: Which tools to use and when. If your problem fits into a broad category, use the first index:

   a)  Find the most appropriate category for your problem.
   b)  Look at the columns on the right to see which techniques work best for the size of group involved in solving your problem.
   c)  Skim through the techniques listed to find the one that looks most appropriate.

If you have a very specific problem, use the second index, which will point you towards techniques that you can use on your own (directly or with a little adaption) or with others.

Remember that you can combine tools and techniques to create even more powerful problem-solving tools.

I hope that you enjoy the book and find it rewarding. I would welcome feedback on your successes, your creative adaptation of the methods, and on the ways in which you have applied the tools in this book.

**David Cotton**
Email: david@davidcotton.co.uk
Web: www.davidcotton.co.uk
Twitter: davidcottonuk

# PART 1

# WHICH TOOLS TO USE AND WHEN

You can use many of the techniques on your own. Some also lend themselves to small group work and some to large groups. For these purposes, let us say that a small group comprises between 6 and 20 people. A large group can be anything from 20 upwards. In 2011, a *World Café* session in Tel Aviv involved 10,000 people. You do not need to think on such a grand scale (just yet) . . .

Whilst many of the problem-solving and decision-making tools are multi-purpose, applicable to a wide variety of issues, some are particularly good for specific purposes. In the table below you will see the category of problem for which they may be useful, the number of the tool or technique and an indication of the size of group that can use it:

One person = you

Two people = small group

Three people = large group

Perhaps unsurprisingly, there are more tools and techniques that can be applied to a wide variety of problems and these are listed below as 'Creative idea generation/ Generic problem solving'.

Many techniques are scalable in terms of the numbers who can use them, and you will see that these are indicated by a mark in more than one column.

Whilst the first index looks at fairly generic types of problem, after it you will find a key to the best methods for solving more specific problems.

# TOOLS FOR BROAD PROBLEM AREAS

| Category | Tool/technique | 🚹 | 🚹🚹 | 🚹🚹🚹 |
|---|---|---|---|---|
| Career planning | 34, 45 | | X | |
| Change management | 1 | X | | |
| | 1, 9, 16, 25, 35, 36, 39, 50, 67 | | X | |
| | 55, 56, 57 | | | X |
| Communicating a solution/decision | 14 | | X | X |
| Conflict management | 16, 34, 59 | | X | |
| Creative idea generation/Generic problem solving | 13, 23, 24, 27, 28 | X | | |
| | 3, 4, 5, 8, 9, 11, 12, 13, 15, 16, 17, | | X | |
| | 19, 21, 24, 26, 27, 28, 30, 31, 32, | | X | |
| | 36, 52, 61, 64, 65, 67 | | X | |
| | 8, 26, 52, 55, 56, 61, 64 | | | X |

(continued)

| Category | Tool/technique | 👤 | 👤👤 | 👤👤👤 |
|---|---|---|---|---|
| Decision making | 7 | X | | |
| | 3, 9, 11, 12, 16, 19, 39, 50 | | X | |
| | 55, 56, 57 | | | X |
| Framing a problem | 38, 54 | X | | |
| | 2, 38, 47, 54 | | X | |
| | 54 | | | X |
| Learning/career development | 48, 49, 50 | | X | |
| Planning | 3, 4, 5, 9, 11, 16, 19, 22, 25, 35, 37, | | X | |
| | 39, 46, 50, 52, 63, 67 | | X | |
| | 46, 52, 55, 56, 58 | | | X |
| Process/system/ product design and improvement | 20 | X | | |
| | 9, 10, 16, 20, 21, 29, 36, 51 | | X | |
| | 57, 66 | | | X |
| Project planning/ project management | 9, 63 | | X | |
| Root cause analysis | 20 | X | | |
| | 20, 32, 33, 41, 42 | | X | |
| Stakeholder management | 22 | X | | |
| | 22, 40 | | X | |
| | 40 | | | X |
| Strategy/ organisational design/ organisational development | 3, 4, 5, 9, 16, 19, 34, 25, | | X | |
| | 39, 52, 60, 63, 67 | | X | |
| | 52, 55, 56, 57 | | | X |
| Testing a solution | 37, 43, 39 | X | | |
| | 10, 18, 37, 39, 43, 59, 65, 68, 50 | | X | |
| | 39 | | | X |
| Time management | 6, 44 | X | | |
| | 44 | | X | |

# TOOLS FOR SPECIFIC PROBLEMS

The index above looks at generic problem areas. Below you will find a handy reference to the tools that will help you to solve some more specific problems. You can use some of the techniques on your own and some will require help from others. In many cases, even though the techniques are designed to be used by people working together, you can adapt them easily to use on your own.

| How can I . . . | Tool/technique | |
|---|---|---|
| | Alone | With others |
| know that I am solving the right problem? | 38 | |
| get more done in less time? | 44 | |
| know that I am spending my work time wisely? | 6, 44 | |
| motivate my team? | 23 | |
| know that I am applying for the right job? | 45 | |
| resolve a conflict at work? | 34 | 59 |
| discover why something is not working correctly? | 20 | |
| know who will be affected my plans? | 22 | |
| ensure that our project plans will work? | | 49 |
| streamline some business processes? | 20 | |
| ever make decisions when senior people constantly over-rule them? | | 8, 12, 52, 53, 55, 56, 57 |
| learn from my peers? | | 10, 48, 49 |
| make change work? | 9 | 1, 16, 25 |
| attract more customers/clients to our business? | 14 | |
| get other people to buy into our ideas? | 14 | |
| design better products? | 9 | |
| ensure that our project plans will work? | | 49 |
| make better decisions? | 7 | |
| see things from someone else's perspective? | 11, 31 | |
| solve a very difficult problem that involves complex relationships? | 26 | 26 |

# PART 2

# PROBLEM-SOLVING ESSENTIALS

# BARRIERS TO PROBLEM SOLVING

There is something rather magical about solving a problem. When you find a solution, often you know instinctively that is the right one – it just feels right. Problems may manifest themselves in many ways, including:

- a discrepancy between expectations and reality;
- failure to meet a standard;
- the need for something to exceed the standard;
- inconsistent results or performance.

There are many reasons why it is difficult to find a solution to a problem. Here are some common causes and brief solutions and, after the table below, you will find more detailed ways of dealing with each issue.

| Cause | Solution (in brief) |
| --- | --- |
| Failure by some to recognise that there is a problem | Help them see the benefits of new approaches and remain non-judgemental about the causes |
| The problem is too big to be solved as one | Break it into smaller pieces |
| Poorly framed problem | Careful framing |
| Solving the problem too quickly | Take time to gather information and understand the ramifications of any proposed solution |
| Politics | Involve the politicians |
| Dominant people | Use methods that soften their voices |
| Lack of understanding of the problem | Thorough research before problem solving |
| Lack of experience among problem solvers | Use methods that allow fresh insights |
| Too much experience among problem solvers | Involve less experienced people with fresh insights |
| Failure to consult the appropriate people | Ensure that you involve those who are affected by the problem and will be affected by the solution |
| Failure to communicate the solution | Ensure that everyone who needs to know is consulted or informed |
| Trying to solve a problem by using the same thinking that created the problem | Use methods that allow you to escape from institutionalised thinking |
| Fixing the symptoms without getting to the causes | Check that you understand the root causes of a problem and attack those, rather than symptoms |
| Others' attitudes! | See the detailed description below |

Let's look at these ideas in more detail:

**Failure by some to recognise that there is a problem:** You may encounter some people who refuse to acknowledge a problem because the admission may cast them in a bad light, or the solution may be uncomfortable. Work with them to see the benefits of a new approach and remain strictly non-judgemental. Some people need to be convinced that continuing to do whatever they are doing will result in disaster before they will contemplate changing.

**The problem is too big to be solved as one:** Break it into smaller, more manageable sub-problems, ensuring that you do not lose sight along the way of the original problem.

**Poor framing of the problem:** You get what you focus on. If you are sloppy in the wording or framing of a problem, you are unlikely to solve it. First, ensure that you are stating the right problem. I have seen many organisations investing time and money in finding brilliant solutions to the wrong problem. If someone asks you to design a chair, the concept of *chair* as you understand it now becomes the anchor point for your thinking. Everything you design will be linked somehow to your current concept of a chair. But what is a chair for? Perhaps you decide that it suspends someone in a comfortable state. Now you are released from the concept of *chair* so you can focus on designing something that a chair is good at. At the simplest level, you may design a hammock. At a more complex level, you may find some way of helping someone to hover, supported by a cushion of warm air. In solving problems, you are *designing* solutions, and you can do this only once you really understand the problem you are trying to solve.

Instead of asking why not enough people buy our products, ask why some people *do* buy our products and why other people buy our competitors' products. What do we do right? How can we capitalise on it? What do our competitors do right? Can we introduce some of their thinking into the enhanced version of our own products and thus take a bigger market share?

Before involving others in problem solving (and, indeed, solving a problem on your own), look very carefully at the way you have framed it. Play around with the wording of the problem statement, and then walk away from it. After some time, return and see if it still feels right:

- Does it capture the essence of the problem?
- Is it too simple? Too complex?
- What would happen if you did not solve the problem? Would anything change?
- Would the problem go away if you ignored it?
- Would a solution to this problem bring other problems in its wake?

**(See the next section for more ideas of how to frame a problem.)**

**Solving the problem too quickly:** Systems thinking theory suggests that the way out of a problem may lead very quickly back in. If you try to solve a problem too quickly with inadequate research or too little understanding of the ramifications of the solution (not only within, but outside your own work area), you may do more harm than good. On the flip side, do not leave an issue unresolved for so long that it escalates or grows bigger.

**Politics:** Sadly, an understanding of organisational politics is necessary in problem solving. You may hit on the perfect solution only to find that you are not allowed to implement it because it does not fit someone's personal agenda. Involving the right people and using methods that give them no greater voice than others and expose them to wider, more popularly held views may help.

**Dominant people:** Many of the methods offered in this book prevent the more vocal, senior or dominant people pushing others towards their solutions. You cannot avoid the person who wants centre stage, but you can choose problem-solving methods that allow them no greater say than anyone else involved in the process. Indeed, some of the problem-solving techniques described here are conducted largely in silence.

**Lack of understanding of the problem:** We did our best to solve it, but did not really understand it sufficiently well at the beginning. Here you need to ask good questions, collect information and contextualise the problem for others helping you to solve it.

**Experience/knowledge level of those attempting to solve the problem:** Take care in choosing people to work with you on solving a problem. There are pros and cons in asking people with a lot of knowledge/experience or too little knowledge/experience, as shown in the following table:

|  | Pros | Cons |
|---|---|---|
| **Too little** | Fresh insight and ideas unconstrained by standard approaches and received wisdom | Too much preparatory work needed to bring them to a level at which they can be helpful |
| **A lot** | They understand the context, the language, the jargon and underlying assumptions or presuppositions | They find it difficult to move away from fixed ideas and standard approaches. They 'know' the answer and are reluctant to entertain alternatives |

**Failure to consult the appropriate people:** If you do not consult those affected by the problem, you may not fully appreciate it. If you do not consult those who will be affected by the solution, you may alienate people and cause bigger problems than the one you set out to solve.

**Failure to communicate the solution:** Solving the problem is not enough – you need to communicate the solution to those who will be affected by it and those who were affected by the original problem. Think broadly here because often an apparently trivial problem and an apparently small solution or decision can have far-reaching effects.

**Trying to solve a problem by using the same thinking that created the problem:** We become institutionalised in our thinking very quickly after joining an organisation. If you apply the same thinking, the same measures, the same assumptions to a problem that its creators applied, then you will have little hope of solving the problem. This book is full of methods that will allow you to escape assumptions and be free to explore alternatives.

**Fixing the symptoms without getting to the causes:** Single loop learning patches over the symptoms – we recognised a problem and we fixed it. Double loop learning explores the root causes of a problem and then fixes the controls or processes that allowed the problem to occur in the first place. If you face a nagging problem at work, discover how it can happen and how you could recreate it, then you will understand how to fix it so it does not happen again. For many years, I led an international team of trainers. When someone made a mistake, I would thank them and ask them how they did it. They were astonished to be thanked, but my thinking was that they had found a way to do something that our procedures had allowed to happen and, far from admonishing for an error, I was grateful that they had exposed a problem in the way that we were working. We discovered the root causes of the problem, resolved them and shared the results as best practice.

**Others' attitudes:** Typical attitudes are:

- 'We've always done it this way.'
- 'You can't do that.'
- 'It's too expensive.'
- 'We haven't budgeted for that this year.'
- 'That's not in our job description.'
- 'Leave well enough alone.'
- 'We haven't got the time.'
- 'We can't spare anyone to work on this.'
- 'Frankly, that isn't our problem.'

There is no single fix here. Be aware of these attitudes and be ready with counter-arguments. Help people to see how much worse off they will be if they fail to tackle the problem. Some will respond to arguments about how their own professional reputation may suffer; others' attitudes will vary enormously and you will have to deal with them at an individual level.

Without becoming too boastful, be sure to tell others what you did to solve a problem successfully or come to a particularly good decision. Share in order to help others foster good/best practice, so they can repeat the success.

Whilst it may be important to include people with a good deal of experience in solving a problem, consider introducing less experienced people into the mix. They may bring fresh ideas and insights that those who 'know the answer' may not have considered. Often, you will find yourself battling against the 'This is not how we do things here' syndrome and many of the collaborative methods in this book help to break down those long ingrained ideas.

We have mentioned already that the way a problem is framed has a significant effect on possible solutions. Let us spend some time looking at how to frame a problem.

# FRAMING A PROBLEM

Einstein is alleged to have said, 'If I had an hour to solve a problem, I'd spend 55 minutes thinking about the problem and 5 minutes thinking about solutions.'

Here are some quick and dirty ways to frame a problem, so that you can solve it.

**40-20-10-5:** State your problem in 40 words, cut it to 20 words, then 10, then 5, to get to the real root of the problem. Sometimes, you will find that concision in framing the problem suggests the solution to the problem.

**Collect information:** Ensure that you have all the facts at your disposal before you begin to solve a problem. Do this particularly if the problem is rather abstract or vague. Once you have amassed information about the issue, be as specific as you can in framing it as a problem question. Consider using this little framework when collecting information:

|   | Problem | Importance | Urgency | Tendency/ Frequency |
|---|---------|------------|---------|---------------------|
| 1 |         |            |         |                     |
| 2 |         |            |         |                     |
| 3 |         |            |         |                     |
| 4 |         |            |         |                     |

*Problem:* What is the nature of the problem?

*Importance:* How serious is the problem considered to be? (e.g. in terms of cost, quality, safety, consistency.)

*Urgency:* How quickly must it be solved before it causes more serious problems?

*Tendency/frequency:* How often or frequently does it occur? Is it getting better, staying the same or getting worse?

**Rephrase the problem:** Keep restating it until it feels right and genuinely conveys what you want to do. For example, you may start with, 'How can we recruit the best people?' Change the verb *recruit* to, say, *attract. Recruitment* sounds like a dreary, form-filling and interviewing process. *Attraction* suggests something altogether more exciting and enticing. Which form of the question do you think would yield more creative solutions?

**Challenge assumptions:** Of course, to challenge assumptions, you have to know what they are. Frame a problem and ask yourself what you know to be true and what, simply, you have assumed to be true. For example, your team members may, regularly, fail to meet their targets. If you focus on making them adhere rigorously to agreed systems and controls in order to meet their targets, you are assuming that the systems and controls are correct and appropriate. You may miss the possibility that the systems and controls are themselves the problem. (You may miss the possibility that *you* are the problem!)

You can expend a lot of time and energy solving the wrong problem. I have worked in training and development for many years and constantly am asked to conduct training needs analyses (TNA). The problem with a TNA is that it presupposes that the answer to a problem is training, where the real answer may be restructuring a department, changing the manager, adjusting or revising a system or process. These are all business issues rather than training issues. I will, happily, conduct a business needs analysis and propose solutions based on business needs, but have not conducted a TNA in more than a decade because I do not want to skew my thinking (nor that of my clients) from the outset.

**Broaden the view:** In focusing on a small, finite problem, you may miss something at a higher level that is causing the problem. By questioning the bigger purpose – the reason for doing something – you may discover that the cause of the problem is not at the level at which you had been looking. Equally, you may be viewing it from too high a level and need to examine it in more granular detail.

**Narrow the view:** Now you have broadened the view and not found the cause of a problem, you may have an inkling that the apparently wide-ranging problem has a tiny, very specific cause. Narrow your focus and see what you can find.

**Change the perspective:** We tend to see issues from a single perspective. By looking at a problem from another perspective – even someone else's perspective – you may gain fresh insights into the true nature of the problem. You may even see the solution without further effort.

**Frame a problem as a question, not a statement:** 'We're not selling enough widgets' is a statement. Asking, 'How can we sell more widgets?' or 'How can we command a bigger share of the widget market?' opens up many more avenues of thought.

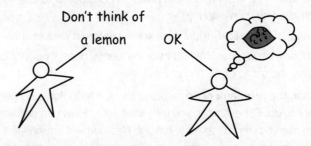

**Frame a problem in positive language:** Negatives are a trick of language rather than something that we can experience. If I say, 'Don't think of a lemon', your natural inclination is to create a mental image of the very thing I have asked you not to think about. Far from removing the thought of a lemon from your mind, I have implanted an image of the very thing I do not want you to think about. Instead of asking 'Why is the team not motivated?' ask 'How can we help our team members to be more motivated?' You will notice, too, that rather than treating the team as an amorphous blob that will be motivated by the same things, we have said *team members,* acknowledging that they may each have different motivational drivers.

**Turn it on its head:** If you are struggling to resolve something, explore instead how you could or indeed *do* create the problem. Rather than asking how to reduce road traffic accidents, consider all the ways in which you and others can create them; then use your answers to stimulate ideas about how you may reduce them. Creativity comes from attacking a problem from a different angle. Throughout the world, town centres are filled with traffic signs. In 2008, the German town of Bohmte received an EU grant to remove its road signs. The only two rules that drivers must obey are a speed limit and giving way to the right, whether to a car, a pedestrian or a cyclist. The number of accidents has reduced dramatically since then. Similar experiments in the UK, Denmark, Belgium and the Netherlands have resulted in a great reduction in accidents. Sometimes, the act of removing rules means that people start to think again for themselves and act more sensibly. If you set out to solve a problem by replacing one control, process or system with another, consider whether you might get the results you want by removal of the control instead.

**SCAMPER it:** SCAMPER is a simple checklist tool for thinking creatively about a problem. It stands for substitute, combine, adapt, modify (magnify or minify), put to other uses, eliminate, rearrange (reverse). You do not have to apply every element of it to your problem, but select the more appropriate ones. Imagine I have a problematic process, a system or a problem, which we will call X:

*Substitute:* Could I substitute something in place of an existing element of X?

*Combine:* Could I combine two or more elements of X to create something more useful?

*Adapt:* Which parts of X could be adapted to resolve my problem?

*Modify (magnify or minify):* Could I modify some aspect of X? Would making part of it bigger or smaller resolve my problem?

*Put to other uses:* Could I take something from somewhere else and use it here? Could I use aspects of X usefully somewhere else?

*Eliminate:* Could I remove some part of X to make it work more effectively?

*Rearrange (reverse):* Could I do parts of X in a different sequence? If I reversed elements of X, would it work better?

Applying SCAMPER to a problem, I may find that the problem simply goes away.

**Focus:** Faced with a series of related problems, be careful to focus on the central or pivotal one. See if one element of the bigger problem is a tipping point. Often, by resolving one small problem, the related series of problems is diminished or even removed. For example, a team is not performing as well as it should, there is a higher than average level of staff sickness and members are failing to fulfil their stated objectives. The organisation determines that a teambuilding event will boost morale, help them to regroup and improve their performance. The real problem is their manager who has been promoted on the basis of technical excellence with little or no equipment to manage. Train or swap the manager and the other problems disappear. Imagine a problem has a timeline: shift your focus from the presenting problem to the time before the problem appeared and look into the future to determine the longer-term effects of the problem.

# STAGES IN PROBLEM SOLVING

Problem solving typically works in six stages:

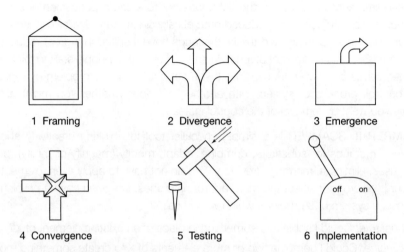

| 1 Framing | 2 Divergence | 3 Emergence |
| 4 Convergence | 5 Testing | 6 Implementation |

Many of the methods in this book follow these stages, sometimes repeating a stage to drill further into a problem.

### PROBLEM FRAMING

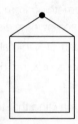

Frame the problem in a way that captures the real essence of the problem and is understood by those seeking a solution.

### DIVERGENCE

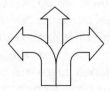

The divergent stage is, for many, the fun and creative stage in which a wide range of possibilities is explored. There are no clear solutions at this stage. If you facilitate it well, you will find that it raises lots of questions and questions keep the door open to learning. Strong facilitation is needed to ensure that there is method in the apparent madness of this stage – keeping people on track and ensuring that they still have the original problem in mind – whilst allowing them the freedom to think around a subject and make free and creative associations with the problem.

## *EMERGENCE*

The emergence stage sees some order begin to emerge out of chaos. The answers that start to emerge are not, necessarily, clearly defined nor thought through in depth but begin to shed light on the problem. It is important at this stage to ensure that the problem solvers remember the initial purpose of their activities and do not pour enormous energy into solving the wrong problem or a different problem. It can cause frustration among those who want (quick) results.

## *CONVERGENCE*

At the convergent stage, participants in the problem-solving process begin to come together in agreement about the best solutions. It may involve evaluating alternative solutions, summarising and categorising key ideas and generating recommendations for action.

## *TESTING*

Check that the solution works. Sometimes, you may have to test it in a small, contained area before applying it more broadly. Often, you will know simply that it works.

### IMPLEMENTATION

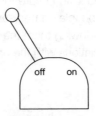

Finally, you put the solution into practice.

# PREPARATION FOR GROUP PROBLEM SOLVING

When you ask a group of people to participate in problem solving, you invite them to risk:

- looking or feeling stupid if their ideas are not accepted by others;
- suggesting things that your organisation may not find acceptable;
- flying in the face of received wisdom about how something is done;
- turning conventional methods and processes on their heads;
- discovering that the way they or others have done something in the past has not been effective or appropriate.

In facilitating problem solving, you have to be sensitive to these issues. Problem solving often results in change and change elicits a variety of reactions from those it affects:

| Active acceptance | Those affected are perfectly happy with the new approach and are prepared to vocalise their acceptance of it | Brilliant! |
| --- | --- | --- |
| Passive acceptance | Those affected are happy to work in the new way and do not vocalise it – they quietly get on and do what they have to do | OK |

| Indifference | Those affected do not care about the new approach. They have seen lots of changes before and one more will not make any significant difference to them | Whatever! |
| --- | --- | --- |
| Active resistance | Those affected vocalise their unhappiness at the new approach and resist adopting it | Boo! |
| Passive resistance | Those affected pay lip service to the changed approach and quietly ignore or even sabotage it | Sure, but not in my lifetime ... |

It is easier to manage each of these reactions if you can identify who falls into each category. Do not simply expect that changes in approach, working methods, systems, controls processes, ways of behaving, etc. naturally will be accepted readily by everyone affected by them. We explore each of these reactions in more detail later in the section on implementing solutions.

# EQUIPMENT NEEDED

For most of the methods in this book, you will need little more than paper and pens, a flipchart (or whiteboard) and marker pens and the occasional sticky note or sticky coloured dot.

In each section you will find a description of what you need. The emphasis throughout is on methods of thinking through problems rather than on the use of technology to resolve them.

PART 3

# PROBLEM-SOLVING TECHNIQUES FOR INDIVIDUALS AND SMALL GROUPS

## TOOL 1 FORCE-FIELD ANALYSIS AND GRAPHICAL FORCE-FIELD ANALYSIS

### WHAT THE TOOL IS

Force-field analysis is a rather pompous name for a pair of brainstormed lists, one describing the forces that will help a change to be implemented, and the other describing the possible barriers to that change. In its raw state, it involves no analysis at all – just listing relevant ideas.

It becomes a powerful tool when the ideas are weighted, either graphically or numerically, showing where we should focus our management effort in implementing the change. The tool can be used by one person or a small group working together, but is best used by one or more small teams of up to six people, working in parallel.

The tool is accredited to Kurt Lewin, a pioneer in social psychology.

### WHEN TO USE IT

- One of the single biggest causes of failure when an organisation plans change is that those affected by the change feel that they have no say in it. Use the force-field analysis as early as possible in the change process, involving as many people as possible who are likely to be affected directly by it. Use it, too, once a high-level change plan has been prepared, to determine the order of priority in the planned steps.

### WHAT YOU WILL NEED

- A flipchart and green and red marker pens.
- A pen or pencil.

### HOW TO USE IT

Divide a flipchart into three columns – two wide columns on the left and right and one narrow column between them. At the top of the left column write *Helpers* and at the top of the right column write *Barriers*. In the narrow middle column write (vertically) a brief description of the proposed change.

Brainstorm all the things that may help to make the change work, and list them in the left column. This should include things that already exist on which you can capitalise or things that, if implemented, would make a positive difference. You may choose to distinguish between the two by asterisking existing helpers. At this point, there should be no discussion, except where clarification is needed.

Brainstorm all the things that may make the implementation of the change difficult, listing them in the right column. Again, you might like to distinguish between existing and possible or anticipated barriers to change. Go back to the *Helpers* column and add any new ideas, repeating the process for the *Barriers* column.

Imagine, for example, that you are brainstorming ways of improving staff motivation.

Note that there is no attempt here to counterbalance each barrier on the right with a helper on the left: the two lists are, relatively speaking, independent of each other, although, in reality, the points on one side will, sometimes, be the reverse of the points on the other.

Using a green marker pen, ascribe weights (strengths) to each *Helper* by drawing an arrow under each one, pointing towards the middle. The length of the arrow (short, medium, long) indicates the strength of the idea. Alternatively, add scores to them to show their relative strength.

Using a red marker pen, ascribe weights (strengths) to each *Barrier* by drawing an arrow under each one, pointing towards the middle. Again, the length of arrow (short, medium, long) denotes the strength of the idea. Alternatively, add scores to them to show their relative strength.

For example, a group brainstorming helpers and barriers to staff motivation may produce something like this:

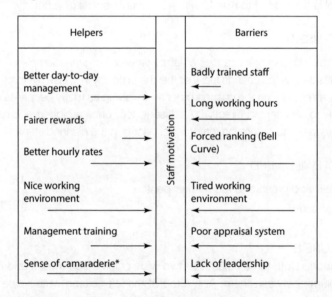

Now examine each of the *Helpers* in turn, discussing how you can capitalise on them to make the change process easier. Start with the items that have long arrows, then see if there are ways to increase the length of those with medium and short arrows, building a picture of everything positive that either exists now or could be done relatively easily.

Then focus on the *Barriers,* exploring how you can reduce or remove them completely, to make the change process more effective. As before, start with the long arrows, then medium, then short.

## VARIANTS

**1** *Two-team version:* Two teams produce the force-field analysis. Using two different flipcharts, team 1 lists *Helpers;* team 2, *Barriers.* Teams swap. Team 1 finds solutions to the *Barriers* and team 2 finds ways of capitalising on the *Helpers* and each shares their ideas with the other.

2 *Graphical force-field analysis:* Two teams produce the force-field analysis, drawing pictures instead of writing words. Often, this engagement of the creative side of the brain results in more imaginative ideas. One person from each team stays with their team's flipchart and the others swap over. The *Helpers* team first must interpret the other team's pictures (aided by the team member who has remained with the flipchart) and then find ways to reduce or remove the barriers that the pictures represent. The *Barriers* team must interpret the other team's pictures (aided by the team member who has remained with the flipchart) and then find ways to capitalise on them. Ideas are shared in a plenary discussion.

## POINTS TO WATCH OUT FOR

It is tempting to believe that the items marked with the longest arrows are the most difficult issues to resolve. In practice, you may find that by removing an obstacle with a short arrow, the apparently more difficult issues resolve themselves, either partially or totally. Sometimes, the smallest issue is a tipping point or lever and its removal may make other problems disappear. For example, a dip in productivity or a fall in sales may be caused directly or indirectly by an individual, whose move to safer pastures removes the bigger, more obvious problems.

## REFERENCE

Lewin, K. (2013) *The Conceptual Representation and the Measurement of Psychological Forces.* Eastford, Connecticut: Martino Fine Books. Reprint of a book first published in 1938.

TOOL 2    # TOUGH QUESTIONS

### WHAT THE TOOL IS

Questions open doors to exploration and creativity. Answers close those doors: often, the moment we believe we have solved a problem, we stop exploring it. *Tough questions* is a powerful tool that helps an individual or team to explore a problem in depth before attempting to find a solution. Indeed, when used well, the technique may throw up questions that have not been considered and change the nature of the problem being explored.

### WHEN TO USE IT

- In the early stages of planning change, exploring an issue or attempting to solve a difficult problem.
- When a colleague has a difficult problem and requires fresh thinking to resolve it.

### WHAT YOU WILL NEED

- Some paper.
- Two chairs opposite each other with a space between them.

### HOW TO USE IT

The technique works best with one or more teams of around five people.

1  One person (the originator) writes down on a sheet of paper a question to which they have found no satisfactory answers.
2  The originator puts the sheet on the floor, sits down on one of the chairs, reads out the question once or twice and focuses on the question, staring down at it on the floor.
3  Others stand around the chairs and consider the question.

4   If the original question prompts a new question in one of the others, they may sit in the vacant chair and ask that question out loud. Nobody must make any attempt to answer any of the questions raised – their job simply is to ask more and more questions. Nobody needs justify their question nor explain why that question should occur to them based on the previous question – participants must accept that the question seemed relevant to the questioner.

5   Anyone can tap one of the seated participants on the shoulder at any time and take their place. When a person is tapped on the shoulder, they must stand up and give their place to the person who tapped them.

6   Once seated, a participant must ask one or more further questions.

7   Continue until nobody has any more questions.

8   At this point, the originator should write down the *last* question asked, read out the original question again and the final question.

It can be incredibly powerful to see how the original question mutates through a series of other questions into something that may, at first hearing, seem unrelated to the original question. Often, the final question has more depth and power than the original and opens up new thinking about the original subject. Sometimes, a transitional question may generate a new stream of thinking and bring insights to the original problem. The person posing the original question may choose to note some of the transitional questions.

## VARIANTS

Use this as a breakout activity in a bigger event. A number of people declare in plenary the questions that they want to explore, each related to the broader theme of the event. Interested parties join them in smaller breakout groups and each group uses this technique to explore the individual questions. In plenary, the owners of the questions read out just the starting and final question from their breakout session. It is interesting to see the reactions of the larger group as the questions are read out.

When the activity is working at its best, the final questions can be quite startling to the larger group and can be the basis of further discussions using other techniques in this book.

## POINTS TO WATCH OUT FOR

Ensure that nobody:

■ tries to answer any of the questions raised but focuses simply on asking new questions triggered by each other's questions;

■ is critical of a question because they cannot see its relevance. It was relevant to the person who asked it.

## REFERENCES

Adams, M. (2009) *Change Your Questions, Change Your Life.* Oakland, California: Berrett-Koehler Publishers.

Pope, G. (2103) *Questioning Technique Pocketbook.* Alresford: Teachers' Pocketbooks.

## TOOL 3    RITUAL DISSENT (AND RITUAL ASSENT)

### WHAT THE TOOL IS

The owner of a problem often has fixed ideas about both the problem and possible solutions. Ritual dissent, developed by Dave Snowden of Cognitive Edge, allows a group of people to discuss a problem whilst its 'owner' turns around and listens to the discussion without intervening. A good discussion gives the owner new insights which, arguably, could not have been gained had the owner taken part in the discussion.

The benefit of ritual dissent is that the problem owner has no opportunity to defend an idea. Whilst this may seem a disadvantage, it prevents the owner becoming proprietorial or defensive about an idea until it has been explored thoroughly by people with less emotional investment in it. This way, the problem owner hears a balanced discussion of the idea and is able to refine it, develop or, perhaps, even dismiss it without first getting caught up in debates which simply entrench biased thinking.

Whilst the technique can be used on its own, it is also a very useful way of assessing ideas generated in bigger collaborative sessions.

### WHEN TO USE IT

- To test proposals or ideas.

### WHAT YOU WILL NEED

- A table and chairs.

### HOW TO USE IT

#### SMALL GROUP METHOD

Use this method when a single idea is being discussed by a relatively small group (say, six to eight people).

1   A small group sits around a table.
2   A problem owner, also seated, presents an idea or an argument in favour of something (e.g. a change, a new way to do something). Usually, the problem owner is given three to five minutes to talk about the new idea.
3   The owner then turns the chair to face away from the table group, who vigorously attack the idea (dissent), find ways of improving it or suggest alternative, better ideas (assent) for a given time (say, 10 to 15 minutes).
4   The problem owner is not allowed to enter the discussion, simply listening to what is said, learning from it and making notes, as appropriate.
5   The problem owner may choose to leave the group after the discussion in order to assimilate the main points, returning later to discuss what he or she has learnt from it.

LARGE GROUP METHOD

Use this method when a number of ideas is being discussed by a large group (sufficiently large to spawn at least three smaller groups with at least three or four people in each).

1   The larger group is divided into smaller, roughly equal-sized groups.

2   Each smaller group sits at its own table, with reasonable space between the tables to ensure that the noise of the discussion about to ensue will not prevent individuals hearing their own table group discussion.

3   Each group works on developing solutions to a problem or issue.

4   Each group appoints a speaker, who is sufficiently resilient both to speak on behalf of the group to another group and to cope with criticism of the group's ideas.

5   Speakers are given some preparation time to assimilate the group's thinking and prepare a brief presentation.

6   Each speaker is asked to stand and move to the next table, clockwise, and take the now vacated seat there.

7   Each speaker presents their group's thinking to the new table. Usually three to five minutes is sufficient.

8   When the time limit is called, the speaker turns the chair to face away from the table group who vigorously attack the idea (dissent), find ways of improving it or suggest alternative, better ideas (assent) for a given time (say, 10 to 15 minutes).

9   The speaker is not allowed to enter the discussion, simply listening to the discussion and learning from it.

10  Speakers leave the group after the discussion and move to a central area to wait until all the table group discussions are complete.

11  Speakers then rejoin their original groups to discuss what they have learnt in the process. Significant ideas may be presented in plenary.

## VARIANTS

If appropriate, you may repeat the cycle, for example:

■ asking the speakers to join a different table to present and listen to the discussion;

■ asking groups to further explore their ideas, informed by feedback from the speaker in the last round, then getting each group to appoint a different speaker to present their refined ideas to a different table group.

## POINTS TO WATCH OUT FOR

■ The problem owners/speakers need to be very resilient.

■ If you have a number of large groups discussing an issue, ask a member of each table group to go with the speaker to the new table group and take notes of the discussion.

■ In facilitating a ritual dissent session, stay away from content – your role is solely that of facilitating the process.

■ Consider whether the table groups should bring together a diversity of experience, views, etc. or whether it would be better to have table groups of people with similar levels of experience or views.

TOOL 4　　# BRAIN-FRIENDLY BRAINSTORMING

## WHAT THE TOOL IS

Have you ever taken part in a brainstorming session and thought, 'There is nothing new here – I could have thought of all these answers myself', then become frustrated that one or two dominant or senior people pushed hard to support their own ideas at the expense of sensible ideas from quieter people less confident in asserting themselves?

Our brains work best on problems at the subconscious level: the 'Eureka!' moment comes when we walk away from a problem. Brain-friendly brainstorming, combined with a technique called PMI (plus, minus, interesting) to sift the brainstormed ideas, overcomes both these problems.

## WHEN TO USE IT

■ To generate ideas to be used in problem solving or decision making.

## WHAT YOU WILL NEED

■ A flipchart and marker pens.
■ A timekeeper.
■ A scribe (who notes the group's ideas on the flipchart).

## HOW TO USE IT

1 State the problem to be resolved or decision to be made. Ensure that everyone understands it.
2 Brainstorm ideas for just two minutes. You may ask someone to keep time for the group. As each idea is called out, it is noted on the flipchart, with no discussion.
3 Stop and discuss something completely unrelated to the problem for a minute or two.
4 Restate the original problem or pending decision.
5 Resume the brainstorming, noting each item on the flipchart as it is called out.

You will find that the most creative and useful ideas will emerge after the short break. The participants' unconscious minds continue to work on the issue, trawling through past experiences to produce better answers.

To resolve the dominance/seniority issue and to arrive quickly at a list of ideas worth further discussion:

1 When the brainstorming session is finished, ask for a show of hands from the whole group for each idea in turn. If the majority believes an idea worthy of further discussion, mark it with a green + (plus).
2 If the majority believes it is not worth pursuing, mark it with a red – (minus). Do not allow any discussion or defence of an idea; if it is outvoted, it is not discussed.

**3** If an idea is deemed to be interesting but not strictly relevant to the current discussion, mark it with a neutral coloured 'i'.

This technique (plus, minus, interesting) comes from Edward de Bono and may also be used to generate new ideas. Very quickly, it produces a list of items worth discussing, regardless of who thought of them.

VARIANTS

If you struggle to write the ideas as quickly as they are called out, the group loses energy. When you are working with a large group of people – say more than 12 – it can be difficult to keep up with the group. Use more than one flipchart, appoint one or more additional scribes to note ideas, and take turns to write the ideas down. On one occasion, we worked with around 30 people, using four scribes and four flipcharts. Each scribe, in turn, would write the next idea as it was called out. This allowed us to keep up with the flow of ideas and maintain the energy in the group.

REFERENCE

de Bono, E. (1985) *de Bono's Thinking Course.* London: Ariel Books.

TOOL 5 # REVERSE BRAINSTORMING

## WHAT THE TOOL IS

Standard brainstorming focuses on how to solve a problem, and the danger is that we bring to it preconceived notions of how something should work. Reverse brainstorming focuses on how to *create* the problem. After determining every possible way to make something go wrong, use the brainstormed ideas as a jumping-off point for thinking about how to get it right.

## WHEN TO USE IT

- When discussion of possible solutions to a problem yields pedestrian answers.
- When you are trying to resolve a problem related to something that people constantly do badly or wrong.
- When you are working with a group of people who have done something the same way for a long time, not considering that it could be done differently or better.

## WHAT YOU WILL NEED

- Flipchart.
- Marker pens.
- A scribe.

## HOW TO USE IT

The technique works best with a group of between 6 and 12 people.

1 State the problem to be solved.
2 Ask the group to call out every possible way of creating the problem.
3 Write each suggestion on the flipchart.
4 When no further ideas are forthcoming, ask the group to use the suggestions to stimulate real solutions to the original problem.

For example:

The problem: *How can we improve the service offered by our call centre?*

| Brainstormed ideas | Solutions stimulated by brainstormed ideas |
|---|---|
| Don't train the staff | Train the staff |
| Take as long as possible to answer the phone Hire staff who have poor language skills | Answer the phone by the third ring Test language skills before hiring |
| Be woefully understaffed | Hire sufficient staff to offer quality service |
| Judge quality by number of calls answered | Judge quality by speed and quality of response |
| Be rude to callers | Be polite to callers |
| Don't share information about problems, trends and solutions across staff | Share information about problems, trends and solutions across staff to avoid 'reinventing' the wheel |

Now use the PMI technique **(see Tool 4)** to determine which of the answers are worth further discussion. Consider using a voting or ranking technique to prioritise them.

## POINTS TO WATCH OUT FOR
Reverse brainstorming is great fun. Just as children love to destroy things they have made, so adults take pleasure in destroying ideas. There is a danger that participants call out silly ideas for effect rather than to help solve the problem. Take care to bring them back on track.

Be careful, too, to steer participants away from simply reversing the brainstormed ideas. A literal reversal may or may not work. Instead, use the brainstormed ideas to stimulate thinking, rather than simply writing the opposite of the initial statement.

## REFERENCE
de Bono, E. (1985) *de Bono's Thinking Course.* London: Ariel Books.

## TOOL 6 PROCRASTINATION

### WHAT THE TOOL IS

This may be the most surprising idea in the book – the idea that you are more likely to solve a problem by procrastinating (putting it off until later). It has been suggested that the most creative people are the ones who, rather than trying to find any quick solution to a problem, dwell on it for a while, leave it and come back to it later when there is more pressure to resolve it. There are several possible reasons why this works, including:

1 Under pressure, you may have to be more resourceful.

2 We solve a problem best when we allow our subconscious to work on it in the background. The subconscious mind goes back through your memory to find similar situations and their solutions, determines the likeliest solution to the current problem and then presents the answer without jogging your memory to remember those situations – the result is a flash of intuition without any conscious rationale for the solution.

Just wait...

Leonardo da Vinci took years to paint the *Mona Lisa,* perhaps as long as a decade. Its slow progress frustrated him, but, in the years in which he carried the idea of the picture around with him and continued to improve it, he studied optics and his understanding of light may have informed his painting – arguably, he became a better artist as he failed to finish his masterpiece.

Psychologist Bluma Zeigarnik noted that people are better able to remember tasks that they have not completed than those that they have. A waiter will tend to remember what diners ordered up to the point at which the bill is presented, and then the order will disappear from the waiter's short-term memory. Zeigarnik said that people were twice as good at remembering interrupted tasks as they were at remembering completed work – the fact that it preys on your mind suggests that your subconscious has continued to work on it in the background.

The cliff-hanger ending to an episodic drama has precisely the same effect as the unfinished task – it gnaws away at us until we see some resolution.

## WHEN TO USE IT

- When you have spent some time staring at a problem, unable to find a solution.

## WHAT YOU WILL NEED

- Pen and paper.

## HOW TO USE IT

1 Start by writing concisely the problem to be solved.
2 Recite the problem statement to yourself a number of times.
3 Sketch a few ideas that may contribute to the solution.
4 Walk away.
5 Return to it occasionally, and attempt to solve it only when you are under pressure to do so.

## POINTS TO WATCH OUT FOR

There is, of course, a danger that you procrastinate so much that you fail to resolve the problem or return to it. You will need a certain self-discipline to make yourself go back to an unfinished task. Still, if Zeigarnik is correct, you will have no difficulty in remembering that the issue is outstanding.

## REFERENCES

Grant, A.M. (2016) *Originals: How Non-Conformists Move the World.* Viking.
Zeigarnik, B. (1938) *On Finished and Unfinished Tasks: A Source Book of Gestalt Psychology* (pp. 300–314). New York: Harcourt.

## TOOL 7    CARTESIAN LOGIC

### WHAT THE TOOL IS

This tool helps a problem owner to explore an issue from all angles. You can use the technique on your own or involve others in the process.

### WHEN TO USE IT

- When you need to ensure that you have looked at the problem from every possible angle.
- When you are torn between two possible solutions.
- When avoidance of the issue could be as useful as tackling it.
- When you want to test a possible solution to a problem.

### WHAT YOU WILL NEED

- Pen and paper.

### HOW TO USE IT

Consider your problem and a possible solution. Let us call the solution X. Ask yourself:

- What would happen if I do X?
- What would not happen if I do X?
- What would happen if I do not do X?
- What would not happen if I do not do X?

    Write down the answer to each question.

|  | *Do* | *Do not* |
|---|---|---|
| **Would happen** | | |
| **Would not happen** | | |

For the logically minded, the questions are based on the statements:

- If A then B.
- If A not B.
- If not A then B.
- If not A not B.

You will discover quickly that the questions lead to similar answers and, usually, the answer to your problem becomes obvious as you work through the questions. Sometimes, the answers raise further questions about your values – what is really most important to you? You may choose to ascribe weights or scores to each element of your moral dilemma, according to its importance to you and use the weighting to select the best answer.

For example:

*I am nervous about giving feedback to a member of my team. He is technically very strong and hard-working, but I know that he is rude and abrasive to other team members (although extremely polite when I am present). I don't want him to lose his enthusiasm for the work, but I do want to create a harmonious team and it will be important for a forthcoming project that he learns to work more effectively with others. Should I tackle him about his behaviour?*

|  | Do | Do not |
|---|---|---|
| **Would happen** | He may lose his enthusiasm | He will continue to be rude |
|  | The team will be happier with his behaviour | He may alienate the rest of the team |
|  |  | He will continue to be enthusiastic about his work |
|  |  | The project will suffer |
| **Would not happen** | His continued enthusiasm | He will change his ways |
|  | The team's continued upset at his behaviour | He will be alienated |
|  | His continued input to the project |  |

The subtle differences in wording in each box take some thinking through. Very often, the method confirms what you already knew, but it is good to have that confirmation. Often, too, the result is not quite clear-cut: the reality in this example is that I should tackle the rudeness issue because it is inappropriate and affecting the whole team. The more basic question seems to be about my management ability! I have avoided talking to someone about inappropriate behaviour because it makes me uncomfortable, and it seems I have decided that the only way my team member can be motivated is by allowing him to be rude to others. The problem of his enthusiasm may need to be tackled as a separate issue. Asking all the right questions helps to clarify the way forward, at least partially, even if the results are uncomfortable.

Here is another example:

*I am ambitious and I enjoy learning. I am considering doing a fast-track, distance-learning one-year MBA, starting next year. It will require me to work around 15 hours per week. I have a full time job, a spouse and a young family.*

Here is a selection of answers to the four questions:

|  | *Do* | *Do not* |
| --- | --- | --- |
| **Would happen** | I will be eligible to apply for a director's post in my firm (all the directors have MBAs) I continue to see as much of my family | I would be frustrated that I haven't advanced either my learning or my career I could never fulfil my ambition of becoming a director |
| **Would not happen** | I would not be able to see as much of my family | I get my MBA I put my family life on hold |

What comes out of this is the moral dilemma: what is more important – career or family? Perhaps the real solution is to consider studying for an MBA over a longer period, so that I can fulfil both ambitions, taking more time with my family and still getting the qualification that makes me eligible for directorship.

## VARIANTS
You can use Cartesian Logic with a group of people who will tend to expand the range of ideas beyond those that you could think of for yourself.

## POINTS TO WATCH OUT FOR
The most important thing here (as with so many problem-solving techniques) is to formulate the right question. It is all too easy to avoid the real issue by skewing the question towards one you *want* to answer or to which you already have an answer, rather than tackling a more difficult question.

The most difficult box to complete is the bottom right (what will not happen if we do not . . .?). It is easy to drift into giving the same answers as in the top left box (what will happen if we do . . .?) and there may be subtle differences that shed more light on the issue.

## TOOL 8   BRAINWRITING

### WHAT THE TOOL IS

This is a very fast, relatively quiet and very democratic method of brainstorming.

### WHEN TO USE IT

- It is particularly useful for collecting ideas from people who are reluctant to offer ideas in a group session or when you need to solve several problems in parallel.
- Use it, too, to prevent senior or loud participants dominating a session – this way everyone gets a say, and in silence.

### WHAT YOU WILL NEED

- Sheets of A4 paper printed with the following headings and a table with as many 'cells' as there are people working on the problems or as many as you can fit on a sheet of A4 paper, still leaving space to write in each cell.

| Problem: | | |
| Owner: | | |
| --- | --- | --- |
| | | |
| | | |
| | | |

### HOW TO USE IT

SMALL GROUP, MULTIPLE PROBLEMS

1   Distribute a brainwriting sheet to each participant.
2   Ask each participant to write their problem and name at the top of the sheet.
3   Rotate the sheets so that every participant has a chance to add one or more possible solutions or the seeds of solutions. Note that if a participant has no ideas about a particular problem, they can simply pass the sheet on to the next person.
4   Continue to rotate the sheets until all ideas are exhausted.
5   Finally, give each sheet back to the appropriate problem owner.
6   The problem owner takes the sheets away to assimilate the suggestions and implement whichever seem most sound.

LARGE GROUP, SHARED PROBLEM

1   Distribute a brainwriting sheet to each participant.

2   Ask each participant to write the shared problem and owner's name at the top of the sheet.

3   Ask each person to write a single idea/solution, complete a row of ideas/solutions or write as many ideas/solutions as they can think of.

4   Pass each sheet to the next person in the group who adds further ideas/solutions of their own and those triggered by others' ideas already on the sheet.

5   When everyone has written something on a sheet, or passed it on if they have no further ideas, give the sheets back to the problem owner.

6   The problem owner takes the sheets away to assimilate the suggestions and implement whichever seem most sound.

## VARIANTS

The same technique can be adapted to large groups with multiple problems and small groups with a single problem.

## POINTS TO WATCH OUT FOR

■ Ask everyone to write as clearly as possible – the problem owner needs to be able to read the solutions!

■ On occasions, someone will query another's idea, declaiming it as silly. Encourage participants to work in silence.

TOOL 9 # INDIVIDUAL AND COLLECTIVE MIND MAPPING

## WHAT THE TOOL IS

We do not think in linear, structured ways, instead combining ideas and making associations. The mind map allows us to organise these connected ideas visually and so sparks new associations. Individual mind maps can help us to solve simple problems.

Collective mind maps, drawn on a large scale, can help us to see new associations as others add their ideas to the picture.

## WHEN TO USE IT

- When you need to think on a large scale, resolving problems whose solutions may have far-reaching effects.
- As a planning tool, to ensure that you have covered all possibilities.
- As a design tool, working in collaboration with others.

## WHAT YOU WILL NEED

- Working alone, a sheet of paper and coloured pens.
- Working with others, one or more sheets of flipchart paper and coloured marker pens.

## HOW TO USE IT

1 Draw a circle in the middle of a sheet of paper, turned landscape, and write a brief description of the problem inside it.
2 Allow yourself to think freely about the problem.
3 As each major solution occurs to you, draw a branch leading from the central circle, and label it with a brief description of the solution.
4 As you think in more detail about each possible solution, draw sub-branches leading from the appropriate branches and label those, too, with a brief description.
5 If you see links between sub-branches, connect them with lines or arrows.
6 Now look at the overall picture you have created and allow it to inspire new ideas, new connections not yet made, new branches and sub-branches. Add them in to the mind map.

If you are working with a group of people, ensure that you have large sheets of paper (flipchart pages attached to a wall are ideal) and lots of space to manoeuvre. Encourage people to take lots of time out to stand back and look at the map as it begins to emerge, so that each person's thinking stimulates ideas in others. Use colourful arrows to connect ideas.

## POINTS TO WATCH OUT FOR

There is a danger that, rather than using the mind map to create free associations and engage the creative side of your brain, you simply use the mind map format as an alternative to linear notes. The power of the mind map lies in our brain's ability to make connections, one idea stimulating another. Rather than explore each possible branch/solution in detail, just jot down ideas as quickly as they occur to you. Notice how branches and sub-branches link to each other and suggest new solutions. If you think it, write it down – do not dismiss an idea because it does not immediately seem sensible. Often, the apparently silly ideas contain the seed of something really useful. To stimulate your whole brain:

- use keywords or key phrases, rather than whole sentences;
- draw pictures in place of, or in addition to, words;
- use different colours for each branch.

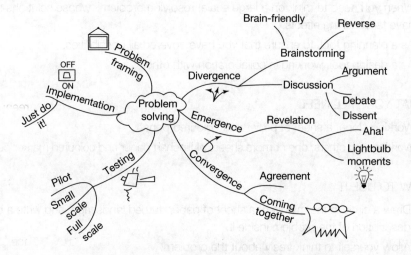

A simple mind map relating to problem solving shows five main branches, each related to the five primary stages, and sub-branches illustrating more detail about each area. Drawings can be useful to trigger key thoughts, memories or ideas.

## REFERENCE

Buzan, T. (2009) *The Mind Map Book: Unlock Your Creativity, Boost Your Memory, Change Your Life.* London: BBC Active.

## TOOL 10 STRUCTURED WALKTHROUGHS

### WHAT THE TOOL IS

When you have an idea of how to resolve an issue and want insights from others, the structured walkthrough can be helpful. In a highly structured way, an audience of interested parties can offer you critical and constructive feedback on your own thinking for you to take away and consider, with no pressure to implement the group's ideas.

The structured walkthrough originated in the IT industry.

### WHEN TO USE IT

- When you have a partly developed solution to a problem.
- When you need constructive criticism to take an idea further.
- When you feel you can benefit from the collective wisdom of others.

### WHAT YOU WILL NEED

- Comfortable seating for the participants.
- An area in which the presenter can present comfortably.
- Check in advance whether the presenter will need a PC, projector and screen; a flipchart; handouts to be printed.

### HOW TO USE IT

One person is the *presenter.* Appoint a *leader* and *recorder*; other participants are *reviewers.* Roles are as follows:

*Presenter:* Presents the ideas and listens to participant feedback.

*Leader:* Chairs the meeting and ensures an egoless approach, an even pace, concentration on the key issues and dictates what will be recorded.

*Recorder:* A non-participant in the discussion, there to record only what the leader asks to be recorded.

*Reviewers:* There to listen intently to the presenter, question areas that they do not understand fully and ask for clarification in difficult areas. Reviewers should be both interested parties and people with no vested interested in the finished solution. They should have sufficient background to understand the subject of the presentation.

1 The leader introduces the topic and, where necessary, the participants.
2 The leader explains each person's role, how the session will work and sets strict time limits.
3 The presenter is there to present an idea, a design, a possible solution but not him/herself.

4　The presenter must present the work in a dispassionate, egoless way.

5　The presenter will benefit from the walkthrough in direct proportion to the selflessness of the presentation.

6　The presenter is there to learn and improve the design, idea or solution.

7　The reviewers are there to assist the presenter by asking questions designed to help the presenter consider other aspects of the problem, explore alternative ways of thinking about the problem, etc.

8　The reviewers must never attack the presenter.

9　The reviewers are there to help, to learn but never to be critical.

10　Alert reviewers will look for loopholes, potential problems and unworkable methods.

11　The reviewers must raise objections as questions to the presenter.

12　The leader must ensure that the reviewers do not attack the presenter and vice versa.

13　The leader must smooth out the presenter's (almost inevitable) feeling of persecution, regardless of the constructive attitudes of the reviewers.

14　The leader must present in a way that concentrates simply on the presenter's areas of comfort or areas in which the presenter has avoided following through.

15　The leader must ensure that the unresolved issues are noted by the recorder in the sequence in which they are raised during the presentation.

16　The leader asks the recorder to record each unresolved point as it arises and read it back immediately so it can be amended, if necessary.

17　At the end of the session, the leader asks the recorder to read out all the recorded points.

18　The recorder's report is given to the presenter not as a definitive plan but as a list of points that the presenter may wish to consider.

19　The structured walkthrough is not designed for decision making. Points raised by reviewers are not considered binding on the presenter.

## POINTS TO WATCH OUT FOR

The leader must be fair and firm, allowing the reviewers space to comment and question, ensuring that the points raised are pertinent and helpful. The leader must be sensitive to the effects of the reviewers' points on the presenter.

## REFERENCE

Yourdon, E. (1978) *Structured Walkthroughs.* New York: Yourdon Press.

## TOOL 11 LIFE THROUGH A LENS

### WHAT THE TOOL IS

Each of us sees life from our own perspective. This simple technique asks you to consider how someone from a different profession would view your problem and how they would begin to resolve it. Seeing a problem through a different lens can give us insights that we would not gain easily from our own perspective.

### WHEN TO USE IT

- When no obvious solution presents itself.
- When your possible solution seems too obvious and you want to see it from new perspectives.

### WHAT YOU WILL NEED

- Paper and pens.
- A large room, if you plan to work with smaller, breakout groups.

### HOW TO USE IT

State your problem. Ask yourself or others, if working collaboratively, how would a(n) X begin to solve it? X may be, for example, an/a:

- doctor;
- lawyer;
- engineer;
- artist;
- statistician;
- politician;
- office cleaner;
- IT technician;
- chef.

Add as many professions as you like to this list, selecting those professions that are sufficiently unlike your own to give you a broader perspective. Stress that you do not expect anyone to understand the detailed work of the chosen professions, instead consider how that person would think about a problem.

For example:

*A doctor might diagnose the root causes of a problem before suggesting a cure; a lawyer might explore opposing sides of an argument before presenting a case; an engineer might explore the detailed workings of an issue; an artist might make preliminary sketches before starting the real picture; a chef might ensure that all ingredients are in place before beginning to create something.*

Discuss which combination of these approaches will guide you towards a better solution and implement the most appropriate.

If you are working with a large group, delegate the appropriate approaches to sub-groups and have them work in parallel on them, presenting to all in a plenary session. For example, one group may compile the balanced arguments for and against an approach, one may sketch a number of approaches and one may analyse the current situation and its likely effects in more depth.

## POINTS TO WATCH OUT FOR

Help participants to understand that the method is not about a literal application of the work of each profession to the problem, but about free association of the characteristics or methods of each profession with the problem. What do they bring to the party that does not naturally fall out from your own way of thinking?

## TOOL 12  NOMINAL GROUP TECHNIQUE

### WHAT THE TOOL IS

A useful technique, developed by Delbecq and VandeVen, to ensure that everyone involved in solution finding has an equal voice. Some believe that nominal group technique (NGT) produces a higher quality list of solutions than brainstorming.

### WHEN TO USE IT

- When a group includes very vocal or highly dominant individuals.
- When you believe that quieter members of the group are reluctant to speak in front of the more dominant ones.
- When the group has, traditionally, not generated a large volume of creative ideas.
- When the issue is controversial.

### WHAT YOU WILL NEED

- Pen and paper for each participant.
- Flipchart and marker pens.

### HOW TO USE IT

1  State the problem and check that everyone understands it. The problem is best voiced as an open question, for example: '*What are some of the ways in which we could encourage employees to come to work on time?*'

2  Individuals silently generate ideas, writing as many possible solutions as they can in a fixed time period (5 to 10 minutes is usually adequate). The facilitator may also write down ideas.

3  In plenary, each participant declares one idea in turn and the facilitator records them on a flipchart:
   a)  No discussion of the ideas is allowed.
   b)  In some versions of NGT, clarification may be sought at this stage. In others, clarification is sought after all ideas are recorded.
   c)  A participant may call out an idea that is not on his or her list, but is inspired by other ideas.
   d)  A participant may decide to pass in a given round and then offer an idea in a subsequent round.

4  Discuss each idea in the sequence in which they are written on the flipchart:
   a)  Members may ask questions and state whether they agree or disagree.
   b)  The facilitator must ensure that each contributor has equal space to talk about their ideas and is not subject to verbal attack.

c) The group may combine ideas into categories and offer new ideas stimulated by what they have heard. The group ranks ideas in relation to the original problem and votes on them. **(See ranking and voting.)**

## VARIANTS

After ideas have been generated and recorded, the facilitator questions whether the ideas are relevant to the stated problem. If they are not, the problem is declared 'ill-structured' because it allowed for responses that were not strictly related to it. The ideas that participants have generated are then clustered into groups – for example, one group would relate directly to the stated problem, another to a different interpretation of that problem. The ill-structured ideas are then regarded as problems in their own right and another round of NGT may be applied to them.

## POINTS TO WATCH OUT FOR

- Ensure that the group really understands the issue being discussed, to avoid ill-structured ideas.
- Ensure that discussion is always calm and constructive and based around the development of ideas and not personal attacks.
- Be careful with the language of NGT. The owner of a problem may feel passionate about it, only to be told that the problem was 'ill-structured'. In their mind, it was probably perfectly structured. You do not have to use the original NGT language.

## REFERENCES

Delbecq, A.L. and VandeVen, A.H. 'A Group Process Model for Problem Identification and Program Planning', *Journal Of Applied Behavioral Science VII* (July/August 1971), 466–91.

Delbecq, A.L., VandeVen, A.H. and Gustafson, D.H. (1975) *Group Techniques for Program Planners.* Glenview, Illinois: Scott Foresman and Company.

# TOOL 13  GROW FOR PROBLEM SOLVING

## WHAT THE TOOL IS

Whilst the GROW model is associated traditionally with one-to-one coaching, it provides a clear framework for problem solving, either individually or collectively.

## WHEN TO USE IT

- When you need a range of possible solutions to a problem.
- When you need to explore a problem in depth and bring something concrete to a partly formed idea.

## WHAT YOU WILL NEED

- Paper and pens.

## HOW TO USE IT

Perhaps the world's most popular coaching tool is GROW, which provides a sequence for questioning the coachee. GROW stands for goal, reality, options, will/way forward. Typically, the coach asks the coachee a number of questions to help the coachee explore a goal, further questions to establish the reality of the coachee's current situation and the possible options available to the coachee based on that goal and reality. Finally, the coach tests the coachee's willingness to continue to work towards the goal and asks which option or options the coachee will undertake first.

The same tool offers a useful framework for problem-solving. You can use it on your own or with others.

*Goal:* Explore in as much depth as you can the problem you are attempting to solve. For example:

- What would happen if you did solve it?
- What would happen if you did not?
- What would it look like, feel like (even sound like) if you had solved the problem? Engage as many senses as possible to make the end goal seem as realistic as possible.
- How would you know that you had solved it?

*Reality:* Explore, again in as much depth as possible, the reality of your current situation and the environment in which you are trying to solve your problem:

■ Who or what might help you?

■ What are the potential barriers or constraints?

■ What might be the indirect consequences of finding a solution?

*Options:* Explore the choices available to you that might resolve the problem. Be as creative as you like at this stage, constantly checking that your possible solutions will actually resolve the original problem and testing the feasibility of your proposed solutions against the reality of your situation.

*Will/way forward:* Given the reality and possible options, do you still have the will to resolve this problem? Which option or combination of the options will you select to start resolving the problem and what will be your first step?

## POINTS TO WATCH OUT FOR
Inexperienced coaches, eager to help their coachees, often dive into solution finding before really understanding the coachee's goal and reality. Equally, when using GROW as a problem-solving tool, you may be tempted to start creating solutions before you have explored the goal and reality properly. Ideally, spend more time on *goal* and *reality* than on the other two categories. When you truly understand your goal and have realistically appraised what will help and hinder you in its achievement, the options will start to appear.

## REFERENCE
The GROW model has been attributed variously to John Whitmore, Alan Fine and Graham Alexander. There are few references to it as a method for pure problem solving. As a coaching tool, there is an abundance of literature. Perhaps the best known is:

Whitmore, J. (2009) *Coaching for Performance: GROWing Human Potential and Purpose – the Principles and Practice of Coaching and Leadership.* London: Nicholas Brealey Publishing.

## TOOL 14  HEAD/HEART-PUSH/PULL

### WHAT THE TOOL IS

Head/heart-push/pull allows you to view the solution to a problem or a decision from all angles so that you can communicate it more effectively.

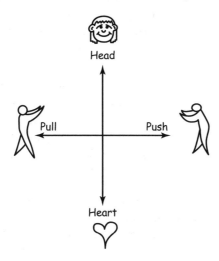

The *head* argument is a rational one, dealing with facts, figures and information coolly and objectively.

The *heart* argument works at the emotional, subjective level, tugging at the heart strings and offering opinions rather than facts.

The *push* approach argues a case so that the listener feels that they have no choice but to comply.

The *pull* approach attracts the listener towards an argument, making it seem irresistible.

By combining head-push, head-pull, heart-push, heart-pull, you can create a set of arguments to convince people from varying standpoints that what you are doing is right for them and for the organisation.

### WHEN TO USE IT

- To ensure that you communicate the solutions to a problem in the best way for different audiences.
- Typically, you would use this at the end of a problem-solving session. You have found a solution to a problem and now you and those who participated in the problem-solving exercise need to consider how to communicate the solution to others.

## WHAT YOU WILL NEED

■ Paper and pens.

## HOW TO USE IT

Either work as a single group or divide the group into four smaller teams, each of which focuses on one facet of communication and then reports back in plenary. The facets are head-push, head-pull, heart-push and heart-pull.

For example: You are a travel agent and you want to entice a couple to buy an expensive holiday from you:

*Heart-pull* – 'Imagine the scene: you are standing on a beautiful beach, the gentle waves lapping at your feet in the soft white sand. Above you, in the azure sky, there is barely a wisp of cloud and a warm breeze strokes your cheeks. In your hand, a cocktail. You haven't a care in the world. And all this could be yours for just £2,550 per person, half board!' The aim is to make an expensive holiday so attractive that the couple cannot resist it, by taking them with you at an emotional level.

*Head-push* – 'On the limited budget available to you, there are only two holidays that you can afford – pony trekking in the Welsh mountains or a city break in Edinburgh. So, if you are restricted to the first week of May, those are your options.' The aim is to push the couple into accepting a holiday at the top of their budget by stripping out any emotional appeal and being absolutely rational.

In reality, you may have to communicate your solutions to a broad range of people, and the trick here is to have considered your communication from all four viewpoints, so that you have your arguments ready and can deal with objections or resistance at a personal level with those to whom you communicate your ideas.

## POINTS TO WATCH OUT FOR

There is a small danger that those working on the *heart-pull* arguments become too dramatic and overplay their ideas. Equally, those working on the *head-push* arguments may risk seeming cold and coercive. Remind participants that this is simply a starting point to consider objections to your ideas or ways of pre-empting those objections to gain more acceptance and that they are dealing with real people here.

# TOOL 15 OSBORN-PARNES' CRITICAL PROBLEM-SOLVING PROCESS

## WHAT THE TOOL IS

A five- (and sometimes six-) step process for critical problem solving. It was developed in the 1960s by Alex Osborn who founded the Creative Education Foundation (CEF) and Sidney Parnes who succeeded him as president of the CEF. Many creative thinking techniques begin with a divergent stage (in which many ideas are generated) and are followed by a convergent stage (in which a smaller number of ideas is selected to address the initial problem). The Osborn-Parnes process is unusual in that it includes divergent and convergent phases at each step of the process.

## WHEN TO USE IT

- When you are faced with a problem that affects a large number of people or a decision whose effects could be wide-ranging.

## WHAT YOU WILL NEED

- A flipchart and marker pens.

## HOW TO USE IT

1 Mess finding (objective finding)

   Challenge yourself at this stage so that you identify clearly the problem to be explored.

   For example:
   - What is the challenge or goal that you wish to explore?
   - What would you like to do or to have?
   - What would you like to improve?
   - In what ways do you work inefficiently?
   - Which relationship(s) would you like to improve?
   - What is currently making you angry or frustrated?

2 Fact finding

   Use the six question words here: Who? What? Where? Why? When? How?

   For example:
   - *Who* is currently involved? *Who* should be involved? *Who* might expect to be involved? *Who* will we deliberately not involve?
   - *What* is happening? *What* is not happening? *What* would happen if . . .? What would happen if not . . .?
   - *Where* does X happen? *Where* does X not happen? *Where* could I make X happen?

- *Why* does X happen? *Why* does X not happen? *Why* do we face this problem?
- *When* does X happen? *When* does X not happen?
- *How* does X happen? *How* can I make X happen? *How* can I stop X from happening? *How* is X a problem?

3  Problem finding

You get what you focus on, and the way you define a problem will have a distinct impact on the solutions you find. At this stage, you should list a number of alternative definitions of the problem. Try prefacing the problem statements with, 'In what ways might I/we . . . ?' Then ask, for example:

- What is the real underlying problem?
- What is the primary objective?
- Why do I want to do X?
- What is my goal in accomplishing this?

4  Idea finding

Use any brainstorming or creative thinking techniques you like here to generate ideas. Avoid criticising or evaluating the ideas at this stage. Your aim is to create the broadest list of possible ideas.

5  Solution finding (idea evaluation)

If you are to select the best solutions, you need to set out the criteria by which you would judge them. Go back to the problem-finding stage to remind yourself of what you were trying to achieve in order to create useful evaluation criteria.

- Set evaluation criteria.
- Evaluate your ideas according to those criteria.
- Select the most appropriate solution(s).

6  Acceptance finding (idea implementation)

Create an action plan to implement the solution(s). Ask yourself, for example:

- Who needs to be involved?
- When will you/they start?
- How long will it take?
- When will it be finished?
- How will you know that you have implemented it successfully?

## POINTS TO WATCH OUT FOR

There is a danger, using this method, of getting bogged down in detail and losing sight of the original issue. It requires strong facilitation and clarity of direction.

# APPRECIATIVE INQUIRY

## WHAT THE TOOL IS

Appreciative inquiry (AI) is designed to orchestrate organisational change. It is based on the notion that an organisation is a socially constructed phenomenon, not a reality. If we can accept that this is so, then changes to an organisation are limited only by our imagination. In essence, we created the organisation based on what we dreamed it might look like and so can change it by that same creative process.

Its originator, David Cooperrider of Case Western Reserve University, believes that traditional problem solving focuses on fixing what *is,* rather than imagining what *could be.* There is no single way to do AI, because Cooperrider was keen that, rather than using one fixed method, those using it developed it in ways that suited them. After all, a single method does not allow those applying it to 'dream' about what could be different, thus flying in the face of the very principles of AI.

AI works on the principle that we should do more of what works rather than focusing on fixing what does not. It focuses on the big picture and on rapid change based on a shared vision of the future.

## WHEN TO USE IT

- For organisational change.
- For strategic planning.
- For community development.
- For building networks.
- For resolving conflict.
- For helping teams to see how to work better together.

## WHAT YOU WILL NEED

- A flipchart.
- Paper and pens.

## HOW TO USE IT

For some years, the most widely applied version of AI was a four-step approach to problem solving, which focuses on:

**Discovery:** Appreciating the best of 'what is' now. The idea is to hold on to the aspects of the object of inquiry that are really worth preserving. What is working well that we should preserve?

**Dream:** Envisaging what might be. What would the organisation, team, etc. look like at its very best? This is often created as a graphical representation of a possible future rather than a carefully wordsmithed vision.

**Design:** Discussing what should be. What concrete proposals can those involved suggest? These are sometimes referred to as *possibility statements* or *design statements.*

**Delivery/destiny:** Innovating what will be. Cooperrider changed the name of the fourth stage from *delivery* to *destiny* because of a concern that the term 'delivery' had connotations of traditional change management. At this stage, participants in the process take actions to make the dream and design a reality. The process avoids the establishment of committees and project teams, encouraging participants to do what they believe is right based around some agreement of the *design statements.*

It is interesting to note that Jan Carlzon, president of the airline SAS in the early 1980s, decentralised power to allow his employees to make decisions and solve problems in the interests of the passengers without first asking for permission. If each of the airline's 10 million passengers came into contact with 5 airline employees for an average of 15 seconds for each encounter, the airline was 'created' 50 million times a year. By taking authorisation away from management and giving it to the employees, he created new *possibility statements* that took a failing airline to 'Airline of the Year' in just three years.

## POINTS TO WATCH OUT FOR
Take care when using AI with some hard-headed business people who may consider concepts like 'dream' and 'destiny' to be a little too New Age or fanciful. You do not have to name the stages in order to use them!

## REFERENCE
Cooperrider, D. and Whitney, D.D. (2005) *Appreciative Inquiry: A Positive Revolution in Change.* San Francisco: Berrett-Koehler Publishers.

# TOOL 17 COMPETITIVE IDEAS

## WHAT THE TOOL IS

Whilst often it is said that the creative juices flow best when you are relaxed, there are times when a spirit of competition can inspire the creative mind. *Competitive ideas* introduces a competitive edge to problem solving.

## WHEN TO USE IT

- Best used with groups of people who are naturally competitive.

## WHAT YOU WILL NEED

- Paper and pens or flipcharts and markers.
- (Optionally) a prize for the winning team.

## HOW TO USE IT

1 Present a business problem to a large group and then break the group into smaller groups.

2 Tell them that they have a set time (as appropriate) to create the best solution(s) to the problem and must present their ideas to the other groups. The solutions must be worked through and feasible. State that this is a competition between the groups to find the best solution(s).

3 After each small group has presented their solutions, groups will vote on the best solution. Groups may not vote for themselves.

4 When the best solution is selected, other techniques may be used to explore in more depth how it can be put into practice.

As a further incentive, you may choose to offer small prizes to the team with the winning ideas.

## POINTS TO WATCH OUT FOR

Ensure that the focus is on quality of ideas, not quantity. In a competitive environment, participants simply may generate as many ideas as possible in order to 'win'.

## TOOL 18  WHY NOT?

### WHAT THE TOOL IS

This is similar to structured walkthroughs but largely conducted in silence.

A solution is presented. Participants try to prove all the ways in which the solution is flawed.

### WHEN TO USE IT

- To test a possible solution to a problem.
- To refine a partly developed solution.

### WHAT YOU WILL NEED

- Paper and pens.

### HOW TO USE IT

1   Present the context of the problem for which you have a notional solution. Explain your proposed solution.

2   Each participant quietly reflects on the solution, only speaking to request clarification where necessary.

3   Participants quietly write down all the reasons why the proposed solution may not work.

4   Participants hand their objections to the problem owner who is not bound by them but may take them away to reflect on them in order to refine the proposed solution or create a new solution.

VARIANTS

1   Participants read out their written objections, then hand them to the problem owner for consideration, without further discussion.

2   Participants read out their written objections and the problem owner may question them but not justify the original solution – this way the problem owner may learn from the participants without becoming proprietorial about the original solution.

3   In a slightly reworked version of *Ritual dissent,* (Tool 3) participants read out and discuss their objections in front of the problem owner, who may listen and take notes but not take part in the discussion.

POINTS TO WATCH OUT FOR

Ensure that participants criticise the solution and do not attack the problem owner who may be sensitive to the criticism.

TOOL 19    **MUSE**

### WHAT THE TOOL IS

This is a staged problem-solving technique. MUSE stands for me, us, select, explain.

### WHEN TO USE IT

- To draw out quiet people who may have something useful to contribute.
- To ensure that those with the loudest voices do not dominate the process.

### WHAT YOU WILL NEED

- Paper and pens.
- A flipchart.

### HOW TO USE IT

1   State the problem and invite questions and discussion to ensure that everyone understands it.

2   Individuals (*me*) silently write possible solutions to a problem.

3   Pairs (*us*) discuss their ideas and challenge each others' thinking to refine the ideas.

4   Pairs now *select* the best of their ideas and post them on a flipchart or poster, visible to all.

5   Pairs *explain* their ideas in plenary.

6   The larger group ranks the solutions and votes on them.

7   The larger group agrees who will implement the solution(s) and by when.

### POINTS TO WATCH OUT FOR

Sometimes a group will assume that the originators of an idea should be the ones to implement it. Ensure that the most appropriate people implement a solution. The most creative thinkers are not, necessarily, the best executors of an idea – design and implementation are two different skill sets.

# ISHIKAWA FISHBONE DIAGRAMS

## WHAT THE TOOL IS

The fishbone diagram was developed in the early 1940s by Dr Kaoru Ishikawa of the University of Tokyo. Though it was designed initially as a product improvement tool, it now has much wider application as a general problem-solving tool, particularly for understanding the many causes that may contribute to a particular result.

Ishikawa believed that quality improvement should be a continual process and that customer service was as important as high-quality products. He worked with Dr W. Edwards Deming, whose work on quality control is represented in this book by his plan, do, study, act tool **(see Tool 21).**

Using the fishbone diagram allows you to see every possible cause contributing to a particular result.

## WHEN TO USE IT

- When a team has fallen into a rut in its thinking about a problem.
- To uncover new connections not immediately obvious through more linear problem-solving methods.

## WHAT YOU WILL NEED

- A flipchart, whiteboard or large pad of paper.
- Sticky notes.
- Marker pens.

## HOW TO USE IT

You can use this technique on your own or with others. The group method is described below. Working alone, substitute 'you' for 'the group':

1 Write down the problem to be solved (the *Effect*) to the centre right of your flipchart or whiteboard.
2 Draw a box around it.
3 Draw a horizontal line from the right of the paper, connecting to the middle of the box.
4 Brainstorm the major categories of possible cause of the problem and write them as branches from the horizontal line.
5 Brainstorm all the possible causes of the problem and for each one, ask 'Why does this happen?'
6 Write each answer as a sub-branch attached to the appropriate category, duplicating the ideas if they logically fit in more than one category.

7   For each cause, ask 'Why does that happen?' and write the answers as sub-causes attached to the appropriate causes.

8   Keep asking why and adding more layers of branches until the group has no more ideas.

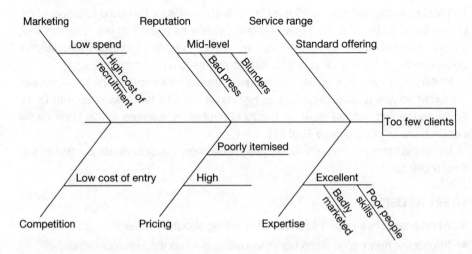

## POINTS TO WATCH OUT FOR

The biggest issue in using a fishbone diagram is to ensure that you have sufficient space on the paper for all the sub-branches. It is frustrating having to start again!

## REFERENCE

Ishikawa, K. (2012) *Introduction to Quality Control*. London: Chapman & Hall.

## TOOL 21 DEMING'S PDSA CYCLE (THE SHEWHART CYCLE)

### WHAT THE TOOL IS

W. Edwards Deming (an American colleague of Kaoru Ishikawa – **see Tool 20**) believed that, through careful measurement and analysis of business processes, it should be possible to determine why products deviate from customers' requirements. He produced a rather simplified feedback loop designed to help managers to identify and modify the parts of a process that need to be improved – the PDSA cycle. PDSA stands for plan, do, study, act.

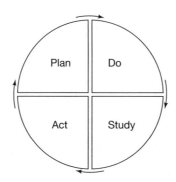

There is nothing very magical about the model – it is a commonsense approach to continual improvement and the real power comes not from using it once but from its constant use. Deming credits his mentor, Walter Shewhart of Bell Laboratories, New York, with the creation of the cycle and referred to it as the Shewhart Cycle. Shewhart referred to it as the PDCA (plan, do, check, act) Cycle. Deming modified it to PDSA.

It is interesting to note that in 'lean' thinking, the *plan* stage is the biggest, whereas in more traditional organisations, the *do* stage is the biggest.

### WHEN TO USE IT

■ In planning for change and continual improvement.

(Note that I have used 'continual' here in place of 'continuous'. Continual implies stopping and starting, whereas continuous means there is no break in the process. Realistically, there is!)

### WHAT YOU WILL NEED

■ No special equipment.

## HOW TO USE IT

Work in sequence through the loop:

*Plan:* Define your objective, and make predictions about the outcome of your plan. Be prepared to answer questions about the plan: Who? What? Where? When? Create or revise a business process to improve results. Determine the data that you will need to collect to measure the success of the plan.

*Do:* Implement the plan and collect data to measure the success of its performance. Ideally, you should test the change on a small scale at first.

*Study (also known as check):* Analyse the data and report your results to the appropriate decision makers. Compare your data to the predictions and summarise what you have learned from the experience and what went wrong.

*Act:* Decide which changes are needed to further improve the process. Plan the next cycle and decide whether the change can be implemented or abandon it if it cannot be made to work.

## POINTS TO WATCH OUT FOR

At first sight, the process looks simple. In reality, being able to predict the outcome of a simple change requires a broader look at everything else on which that change may have an impact – do not just look at the splash as you throw a stone in water, but look at the more distant effects of the ripples after the splash. If you are going to use Deming's method, then you need to commit to it over the long term. It is an iterative process and you should work on a small scale before making wide-ranging changes. Involve as many people as you can, even in the smallest of changes, to reduce the barriers to changes that will affect many people.

## REFERENCE

Deming, W.E. (2000) *Out of the Crisis.* Cambridge, Massachusetts: MIT Press.

TOOL 22 3D STAKEHOLDER MAPPING

## WHAT THE TOOL IS

In any major project or business change, it is essential to identify and manage the stakeholders – those with a vested interest in the issue. The standard two-dimensional stakeholder map is often filed away and not consulted during the lifetime of the project or change. The three-dimensional stakeholder map is constructed using a grid marked on the floor and real people who take positions in the grid, according to the level of influence, anticipated level of support and effect of the project or change on the person or stakeholder group that they represent.

In bringing the map to life, you can increase greatly the chance that the map will be used dynamically to ensure that stakeholders are appropriately managed.

## WHEN TO USE IT

- At the start of any project involving multiple stakeholders.
- At the start of any major change programme.
- When there are complex relationships between stakeholders.
- When you need to understand the best ways to influence stakeholders.

## WHAT YOU WILL NEED

- Duct tape.
- A4 paper and marker pens.
- A ball of string and a pair of scissors.
- A room with plenty of space.
- A camera or mobile phone with camera.

## HOW TO USE IT

1 Bring together a team that has a role in implementing the project or major change.
2 Use duct tape to create the grid shown. Mark the axes and scales using paper labels. Squares/cells must be big enough to accommodate several people.
3 Brainstorm the names of each individual or group with a vested interest in the project or change.
4 Write each name in big, bold letters on a separate sheet of paper and distribute the sheets to participants.
5 Each participant must, with the group's agreement, move into the appropriate square/cell in the grid for the stakeholder they represent and hold up the piece of paper showing the name of the stakeholder they represent.

6   They should stand, kneel or sit according to the expected level of impact of the project or change on the stakeholder they represent (stand=high, kneel=medium, sit=low).

7   If a stakeholder is where we would want them to be (e.g. in terms of support or influence), then leave them as they are.

8   If the project or change would be easier to manage if a stakeholder occupied a different square, ask the participant representing that stakeholder to point to the ideal square for that stakeholder – the square in which that person would offer the most help or cause the least damage to the change or project.

9   If any of the participants believe that they are in a position to influence the stakeholder to change his/her mind and move to a different square, leave them as they are. If not, identify someone else in the grid, known to the participants, who could influence them to move. Attach the influencer and errant stakeholder to each other with a piece of string.

10  When everyone is in place, hands are pointing and string is attached, either take photographs of the 3D grid from every possible angle or sketch the map on a piece of flipchart paper.

Now there are two possibilities:

1   Disband the group and send the photos to each participant. Use prints of the photos at each project meeting to manage stakeholder relationships.

2   Use the flipchart map immediately in planning how the group will manage stakeholder relationships.

## POINTS TO WATCH OUT FOR

■ Initially, some of those involved in creating the map may think that standing, kneeling or sitting in a grid on the floor is silly and do not want to be involved in it. Typically, the moment one person steps into the grid, others follow.

■ Stakeholder maps are dynamic tools and will change throughout a project or change programme. Physical involvement in the creation of the map tends to impress upon the participants the importance of proper stakeholder mapping and management, but they need to understand that the map will change constantly and that they have a role in making it change, as they work to influence the appropriate stakeholders, whether directly or indirectly.

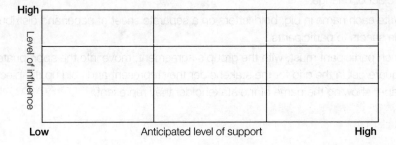

## TOOL 23 THE TWO WORDS TECHNIQUE

WHAT THE TOOL IS

A tool that uses free association of words relating to a problem to create fresh insights into the problem.

WHEN TO USE IT

- To create fresh insights into a problem or to inform a decision.

WHAT YOU WILL NEED

- Pen and paper.

HOW TO USE IT

1 Create a two-word phrase to summarise a problem.
2 Write each word at the head of a column in a table and then freely associate ideas with each word, listing them in the table columns.
3 Randomly match pairs of words across the columns to gain new insights into the problem and its possible resolution.

For example:

I manage a team of 20 people whose motivation levels fluctuate and vary from highly motivated all the time to hardly motivated any of the time (and all possibilities in between). I want to know how I can create higher levels of motivation for more of the time. I create a table, headed with the words 'Staff' and 'Motivation' and make free associations with those words, writing my thoughts in the appropriate columns. I then create random pairings of words to see what new ideas emerge:

| Staff | Motivation |
|---|---|
| Diverse | Happiness |
| Teams | Reward |
| Individuals | Recognition |
| Clever | Gifts |
| Difficult | Parties |
| Busy | Challenge |
| Lazy | Recognition |
| People | Achievement |

Let us say I randomly pair the words 'individuals' and 'recognition'. Am I showing individuals the recognition they deserve, commensurate with effort? Am I showing favouritism (too much recognition) to some at the expense of others?

Now I pair 'lazy' and 'challenge'. Am I giving people sufficiently stretching work to stimulate them? Are the ones I deem to be lazy actually efficient workers who complete their workload more quickly than others? Am I considering some to be lazy who would work better if they understood more of the context of their work and its importance to others?

I pair the words 'diverse' and 'achievement'. Am I too focused on one specific aspect of the team's work, favouring those who excel in that area and neglecting other areas of excellence and achievement simply because it has not been on my radar?

I pair the words 'busy' and 'happiness'. Have I been too busy doing my own work for purposes of self-fulfilment (happiness) to pay sufficient attention to members of my team?

As you make these random pairings, so they stimulate questions and those questions open the doors to new learning.

## POINTS TO WATCH OUT FOR

Do not assume that, because a question arises from these random pairings, that you must answer it and that it has deep significance. Equally, do not be too quick to dismiss a question because it makes you feel uncomfortable. The best questions are the ones that cannot be answered quickly – the greater time you find yourself thinking about the answer, the better the question.

## TOOL 24 THE ASSOCIATION GRID

### WHAT THE TOOL IS

This is an extended version of the *two words* technique **(see Tool 23)**.

### WHEN TO USE IT

- As for the two words technique, to create fresh insights into a problem or inform a decision.

### WHAT YOU WILL NEED

- Pen and paper.

### HOW TO USE IT

Create a table of five or six columns and rows. Think about the problem to be solved and, as you begin to associate words or ideas with the problem, write them in the table cells, one per cell, in any sequence. Now combine ideas randomly from the table, and new and creative solutions to the problem will begin to emerge.

For example:

*You are overwhelmed with work at the moment. Your boss assures that you that the situation is temporary and that, as soon as a new team member is hired, your workload will be reduced again to more normal levels.*

| stress | headaches | resilience | overload | respite |
|--------|-----------|------------|----------|---------|
| overworked | unfair | pressure | unsupported | help |
| delegation | protection | resign | priorities | support |
| drowning | important | urgent | logjam | nightmare |
| solutions | unmanageable | exhausted | strained | overloaded |

Now, combine words randomly and see what insights emerge.

For example, I combine 'urgent', 'important' and 'priorities'. Using Covey's time management matrix, I can start to prioritise my work in terms of what is/is not urgent or important:

|  | *Urgent* | *Not urgent* |
|--|--------|------------|
| Important | 1. | 2. |
| Not important | 3. | 4. |

Anything deemed to be urgent and important goes into box 1; anything important and not urgent goes into box 2, etc. I know that I should execute the work in sequence – box 1, then 2, then 3 then 4 and that the bulk of my work should be in box 2, where I can plan it properly. What tells me that something is urgent? Whose sense of urgency is it? If someone tells me something is urgent, a good question to ask is, 'Which part of this is urgent?' Often, a small part is important and urgent (box 1) and the rest belongs in box 2, where I can take a little more time over it. Many things stop being urgent the moment that they are delegated to someone else. Perhaps I have more time to do them than I thought?

Now let us look at the word 'delegate' and combine it with 'overloaded' and 'nightmare'. Which team members can I trust? What would happen if I approached them and said, 'I'm having a nightmare at the moment. I am covering for X who has left and I'm overloaded with work.' Ask them if they can help, even with small things, which would allow you to concentrate on the bigger issues.

Combine 'unsupported' and 'logjam'. Think about your standard working hours and how much overtime work you can feasibly do. Prioritise your work, using the Covey matrix or another favourite method and discover where the real logjams are. Is there anything that, if it could be completed, would free up a significant amount of time to tick a number of other items off your list? Consider how you could approach your boss a second time and explain that you are feeling unsupported at the moment. (It may be more useful to reframe it in terms of needing support rather than the more accusatory-sounding 'unsupported'.) Show your prioritised list and ask your boss to take some time to work through it with you, asking if there are others who could take on some of your excessive workload.

You will notice that, in this example, the solutions that begin to present themselves are largely commonsense. When you are overwhelmed, it can be difficult to see a situation rationally, and the *association grid* may help to clear the fog and bring some objectivity to the problem.

## POINTS TO WATCH OUT FOR
Do not expect every word or combination of words to suggest a new insight or solution. Make associations as freely as you can with the problem at the outset; even if it is not clear to you why a word should be relevant to the problem, write it down anyway. Then be as free as you can in making associations between the combined words in the grid and the original problem. The most off-the-wall ideas often spring from the subconscious in surprising ways to create new approaches to a difficult situation.

## REFERENCE
Covey, S., Merrill, A.R. and Merrill, R.R. (1994) *First Things First: To Live, to Love, to Learn, to Leave a Legacy.* New York: Simon and Schuster.

TOOL 25  # THE DELPHI TECHNIQUE

## WHAT THE TOOL IS

This is a technique that allows experts to forecast probabilities and possibilities anonymously in a number of structured rounds, each time refining ideas based on inputs from others. It was designed in the 1950s by Dalkey and Helmer of the Rand Corporation. Experts exchange views via an anonymous questionnaire or survey, independently reporting to a facilitator who collates and summarises those views. Subsequent questionnaires allow the experts to dig deeper, refine their ideas and reach consensus. The anonymity of the process allows them to save face, should they change their views.

## WHEN TO USE IT

- When you want to know with some certainty the likelihood and outcome of future events. For example, as a project manager, what future events may have an impact on your projects?

## WHAT YOU WILL NEED

- Time and patience! (This is the slowest technique in the book.)

## HOW TO USE IT

1  Appoint a facilitator. Ideally, this should be someone with a background in research and data collection.
2  Identify a team of experts – people with relevant knowledge and experience of the topic you are going to discuss.
3  Define the problem to be solved. Create a clear, comprehensive definition of the problem in language that the chosen experts will understand.
4  *Round one:* Distribute an open-ended questionnaire to begin the process of collecting information about a specific area of content. Collate the responses and summarise them, removing irrelevant material and checking for common viewpoints.
5  *Round two:* Create a new questionnaire based on the responses to the first, designed to explore the topic in more depth. Once more, collate the responses and summarise them, removing irrelevant material and checking for shared viewpoints and common ground.

**6** *Round three:* Create and distribute a third and final questionnaire, designed to support decision making. What have the experts agreed on in their responses to the first two questionnaires? (You may choose to create further questionnaires if it is necessary to achieve consensus.)

**7** Analyse the findings from the final questionnaire, and plan actions based on the consensus views.

## POINTS TO WATCH OUT FOR

Even when exploring a relatively simple situation, the Delphi Technique is slow, so allow time for it. Be extremely careful in defining the initial problem. Experts like to be right and can be quite pedantic – if they see a fault in the definition or the process, they may exploit it and so sabotage the process. They may be slow to respond to questionnaires because they are busy or because the subject matter does not seize their imagination.

## REFERENCES

Dalkey, N.C. (1969) 'An Experimental Study of Group Opinion', *Futures,* 1 (5), 408–26.

Dalkey, N.C. (1972) 'The Delphi Method: An Experimental Study of Group Opinion' in Dalkey, N.C., Rourke, D.L., Lewis, R. and Snyder, D. (Eds.) *Studies in the Quality of Life: Delphi and Decision-making* (pp. 13–54). Lexington, MA: Lexington Books.

Dalkey, N.C. and Helmer, O. (1963) 'An Experimental Application of the Delphi Method to the Use of Experts', *Management Science,* 9 (3), 458–67.

TOOL 26  # THE LOTUS BLOSSOM TECHNIQUE

## WHAT THE TOOL IS

The Lotus Blossom technique, invented in Japan by Yasuo Matsumura, combines brainstorming and mind-mapping to create an extensive graphic that explores many aspects of a problem in a way that combines structure with creativity. It is not only elegant but can reveal complex relationships and depth that do not necessarily emerge from more standard brainstorming techniques.

## WHEN TO USE IT

- When standard brainstorming techniques would not give depth of solution.
- When you want to explore relationships between components of a problem.

## WHAT YOU WILL NEED

- Flipchart paper and marker pens.

## HOW TO USE IT

1  Draw a 3x3 grid in the centre of the page. This is grid 1, which represents the central problem to be solved or the issue to be explored. In the centre of the grid, write a word or phrase that summarises the problem to be explored:

|  |  |  |
|---|---|---|
|  | **Core idea** |  |
|  |  |  |

Each of the cells around the centre will represent a sub-topic of the main idea.

2  Brainstorm solutions, related concepts or ideas, and write a keyword description of each in the boxes surrounding the problem in the central grid. You may struggle at first to suggest eight related ideas, but persevere – the greater the detail, the richer the solution and the greater the number of associations you will

see between ideas. For our purposes, we have simply lettered the subtopics A–H:

| A | B | C |
|---|---|---|
| H | Core idea | D |
| G | F | E |

3   Around the central grid, draw 8 more 3x3 grids – grids A to H (3 above, 3 below, 1 to each side). Each of these grids will be used to further break down the subtopics, A–H.

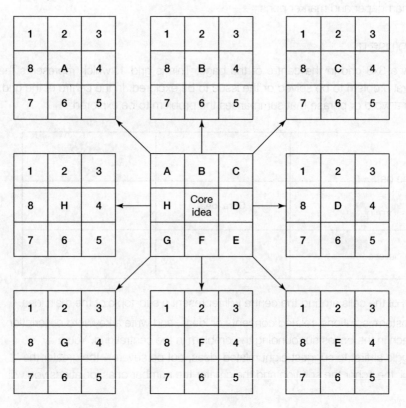

4   Take each of the words that you wrote in the central grid (in our case, A–H) and put those words in the centres of the surrounding grids. The diagram will show you how this would look.

**5**  For each of the eight grids, brainstorm ideas related to its central theme and write them in the boxes surrounding the central idea. In our diagram, we have simply numbered them 1–8 for each grid. In reality, you would have eight sub-sub topics per grid.

**6**  When you have finished, you will have 64 ideas to help solve the original problem. They will vary in usefulness and importance and you may find that just one or two suggest the best solution. However, by looking at the problem broadly, you may start to identify the ripple effects of a solution across other aspects of your operations or organisation.

The problem – *We want to improve our customer service at a call centre which is central to our operations.*

In the central grid, we write *Call centre* and then brainstorm ideas related to the call centre:

| Monitor repeat contact | Customer feedback | Sharing information |
|---|---|---|
| Proactive not reactive | **Call centre customer service** | Faster response times |
| Incentives | Customer contact preferences | Staff training |

Each of these ideas now becomes the central idea in boxes A–H. Now we need to brainstorm ideas in each of the grids.

Let us look at box C. In the centre, we write *Sharing information.* The concept here is that the better the information sharing among call centre staff, the less duplication of effort and the better they can offer a quick and consistent service to callers.

Brainstorming *Sharing information* yields the following ideas . . .

| Share clever solutions | Train each other | Use intranet |
|---|---|---|
| Share best practice | **Sharing information** | Publish FAQs |
| Email tips to super-users | Create customer web forum | Create staff manual |

Repeat the process for each major idea in the central grid. Now you have a wealth of ideas to help focus your management effort in call centre improvement.

## VARIANTS

To complete the 8 grids requires you to think of 64 ideas, which may, at first, seem daunting. In reality, it is not unusual to generate 64 ideas in a brainstorming session, and the Lotus Blossom technique gives a structure to the thinking that is lacking in more traditional brainstorming – you are finding only eight new ideas under eight headings!

■ If you are working with a group of people, break it into smaller groups, with everyone involved in the plenary discussion about the eight main areas, then each group working on one or two of the subtopics. You might consider printing nine separate blank grids – one for the core topic and one each for the subtopics. Distribute the blank grids to smaller groups. Working on a 9x9 grid may seem less daunting than working on the full nine-grid model. When each subgroup has finished, put the pieces together and fix them to a wall so everyone can see the completed picture. One word of warning here: when everyone works on the grid together, they start to see and make connections whilst constructing the overall set of grids. If the smaller groups work in isolation from each other, it may reduce the number of creative connections and the end result may not be as effective.

But:

■ Consider using something other than squares in your grids. In line with the name Lotus Blossom, some people create a flower, writing the topic at the centre and the subtopics on the surrounding petals.

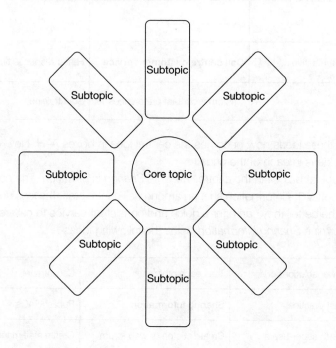

## POINTS TO WATCH OUT FOR

The better the ideas generated in the central grid, the better the overall solution will be. Spend a little more time getting the first grid right, and the rest should flow relatively easily from there.

## TOOL 27 PHOTOGRAPHIC ASSOCIATIONS

### WHAT THE TOOL IS

Often, when solving a problem, we look at the most obvious causes and miss the real underlying issues. *Photographic associations* is a creative tool in which we make associations between randomly selected photographs and the presenting problem. As we make more creative or even outlandish associations, so solutions to the original problem will start to emerge.

### WHEN TO USE IT

- With creative, imaginative groups.
- With groups who are bored with more conventional brainstorming techniques.

### WHAT YOU WILL NEED

- A selection of photographs with no particular, obvious relationship to each other.

### HOW TO USE IT

1 State the problem to be solved/the issue to be explored.
2 Distribute a number of photographs among participants. Ensure that there is a diverse range of subject matter in the photos.
3 Ask participants to make free associations between the images in the photos and the problem and to document those associations.
4 In plenary, ask participants to call out their ideas and use others' solutions to stimulate further ideas.
5 When all solutions have been suggested, use PMI **(see Tool 4)** to sort them, or a voting/ranking technique to prioritise them.

### POINTS TO WATCH OUT FOR

As with many other creative techniques, there is a danger that the more process or logic-minded will try to make literal connections between the photos and the presenting problem. Stress that the associations should be as free as possible to stimulate thinking and to help the creative side of the brain to make associations that would not emerge from head-on, logical approaches to the problem.

### REFERENCE

Tanner, K. and Cotton, D. (2006) *Picture This.* Altrincham: Wize-Up Ltd.

TOOL 28  # THE RANDOM WORD TECHNIQUE

## WHAT THE TOOL IS

Like *Photographic associations,* the *Random word* technique allows us to make free associations between something apparently unrelated to the presenting problem and the problem itself, giving creative insights not accessible using more linear problem-solving methods.

## WHEN TO USE IT

■ When you need to look beyond the obvious for a solution.

## WHAT YOU WILL NEED

■ Paper and pen or flipchart and marker pens.

## HOW TO USE IT

State the problem to be solved. Select a random book, random page and random line number. Find the first noun on the chosen line and write it on a flipchart. Ask the group to call out anything they associate with the chosen word – it does not matter how outlandish their suggestions are – in fact, the more creative, the better. Write each word or phrase on the flipchart as it is called out. There should be no discussion at this point.

When no further ideas are forthcoming, restate the original problem and ask the group to freely associate the brainstormed ideas with the original problem. They can combine the ideas to form new associations with the original problem.

For example:

*A restaurant owner is concerned that, because of the location of her restaurant, she is not attracting the volume of trade she needs. Although the restaurant is in the centre of a major city, it is on a side-street off a main shopping street from which it is not visible. She wants as many ideas as possible of how to attract more people to the restaurant.*

After selecting a random book, page and line, the first noun on the line is *hammer*. The group's suggestions include:

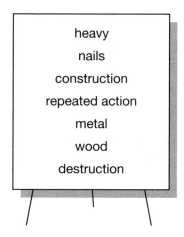

heavy

nails

construction

repeated action

metal

wood

destruction

The group now starts to associate the ideas freely with the original problem. Ideas include:

- Heavy metal and other themed music nights to attract different audiences (*heavy* and *metal*).
- Children are given pizza bases and a variety of toppings and encouraged to decorate the pizzas themselves, which are then cooked and served (*construction*).
- Greek-themed evenings with Greek food, music and plate smashing (*destruction*).
- Loyalty cards offering a free meal after each six purchased (*repeated action*).
- Beautician offering manicures/pedicures before lunch (*nails*).

## POINTS TO WATCH OUT FOR
Participants may, at first, try to make logical links between the random word associations and the original problem. Help them to understand that the power of the technique comes from free association and combining ideas to make new associations.

## REFERENCE
de Bono, E. (2009) *Lateral Thinking: A Textbook of Creativity.* London: Penguin.

## TOOL 29 CHALLENGING ASSUMPTIONS

### WHAT THE TOOL IS

This is a simple and powerful creative tool. List everything you know about something familiar, then treat every statement as an assumption, finding alternatives to the apparently obvious.

### WHEN TO USE IT

- When you feel constrained by a system or process.
- When you feel that a design is becoming old and tired.

### WHAT YOU WILL NEED

- Flipchart and marker pens.

### HOW TO USE IT

1 Ask the group to call out everything that they know about the current object of the discussion. What are the attributes of the current version? List each answer on a flipchart.
2 Now ask them to consider that none of these attributes is real nor cast in stone – each is simply assumed to be real.
3 For each attribute listed, ask them to suggest one or more alternatives.
4 Draw together the alternatives and see what you could create.

For example:

*Imagine going back in time to the days of desktop telephones. What were the standard attributes of the early telephone?*

They might include these:

Substitute something new for each of these attributes:

- It had a dial – change to a touch screen, push buttons or voice control.
- It had a separate base and handset – combine them into a single unit.
- It was static – make it portable.

- It was heavy – make it light.
- It had wires – make it wireless.
- It rang when someone called you – make it play music or flash a light.

In the space of a few minutes, you have 'created' a mobile phone!

## POINTS TO WATCH OUT FOR

Some participants will object to change from the outset, claiming, 'You can't do that!' simply because they have always done something a particular way and a change takes them out of their comfort zone. Others may want change simply for the sake of change. Strong facilitation is needed to keep ideas flowing and ensure the group strikes a good balance between conservatism and outlandish suggestions.

## TOOL 30 METAPHORICAL PROBLEM SOLVING

### WHAT THE TOOL IS

Sometimes, when we tackle a problem head-on, we struggle to find creative solutions. This technique involves finding something analogous to the problem to be solved, brainstorming ways of solving the analogous issue, then 'back-mapping' those solutions to the original problem.

### WHEN TO USE IT

- When more conventional 'head-on' problem-solving techniques have yielded pedestrian solutions.

### WHAT YOU WILL NEED

- Flipchart and marker pens.
- Paper and pens.

### HOW TO USE IT

1 State the problem.
2 Invite participants to suggest a different problem that is analogous to the presenting problem.
3 Find solutions to the metaphorical problem.
4 Map these solutions freely back to the original problem.
5 Select from the 'back-mapped' ideas, those that have merit.

*For example:*

1 Attracting more customers/clients – catching fish.
2 Developing our business – growing plants and flowers.
3 Reducing the bureaucracy at work – weeding the garden.

Let us take example 3 – reducing the bureaucracy at work.

*Step 1*   The problem is that we have too much form-filling to do at work. There is a sort of trivial rigour surrounding even the most mundane tasks. Everything requires several levels of authorisation. We seem to spend more time on red tape than actually doing our jobs.

*Step 2*   The chosen analogy is weeding the garden.

*Step 3*   Now we have to brainstorm ways of clearing the weeds from the garden. Ideas might be:

- Turn over the soil to expose the roots of the weeds, to make them easier to clear.
- Use weedkiller.
- Dig out the offensive weeds.
- Ensure that, as we dig out the weeds, we retain the flowers that we want to keep, etc.

*Step 4*   Now we need to 'back-map' the new solutions to the original problem. The trick here is to do it fairly freely, not trying to find an exact match. For example:

- Turn over the soil to expose the roots – do a thorough review of existing policies and procedures and sift out those that are neither valid nor workable.
- Use weedkiller – be ruthless in removing useless administrative procedures, retaining nothing simply because it is the way we have always done things.
- Dig out the offensive weeds – this really repeats earlier ideas. That does not matter at all in this process because, often, a repeated ideas suggests a certain strength of feeling behind the idea. If it feels like the right thing to do, then it most probably is.
- Retain the flowers we want to keep – be careful not to be so ruthless that we throw away useful policies and procedures.

The example is a relatively straightforward one. Somehow, by taking a metaphorical view of a problem, the discussion can become less emotive because it is held, effectively, at arm's length. Then the decisions that fall out of the discussion will seem easier to execute.

## POINTS TO WATCH OUT FOR

Some people struggle to make the leap between a metaphor and the situation that it represents. They may try to create literal associations between the metaphor and the problem. Encourage them from the start to be free-ranging in their thought, using the metaphor as a jumping-off point for thinking, rather than an exactly mapped parallel universe!

TOOL 31

# WHO ELSE HAS SOLVED THIS PROBLEM?

## WHAT THE TOOL IS

There is little point in spending time solving a problem that has already been solved elsewhere. This technique is about determining where our current problem may also be a problem for others and how they have resolved it. What can we learn from them? It does not matter if our problems and theirs are not absolutely identical – what matters is that they have found solutions from which we can learn.

## WHEN TO USE IT

- When we need a solution in a hurry.

## WHAT YOU WILL NEED

- Paper and pens.
- Flipchart and marker pens, if working with a larger group.

## HOW TO USE IT

1 State the problem.
2 Setting aside the specific context in which the problem occurs in our organisation, list those who, at a more generic level, have had to face this or a very similar problem. You may consider direct competitors, similar organisations or even organisations or individuals unrelated to your area of work who faced something similar.
3 What did they do to solve the problem?
4 How can we, either directly or with some tailoring, adopt the same solution(s)?

For example:

*An IT repair company asks how it can respond more quickly to its customers in order to offer better and quicker service.*

*The analogy – doctors' management of waiting times for patients.*

List what the doctors do to solve their own problem and, against each solution, write tailored solutions for the IT repair company:

| Doctors' solutions | IT repair company solutions |
| --- | --- |
| See customers strictly in order of call | Ticketed waiting system |
| Triage system | Rank repairs by urgency or other criteria |
| Touch-screen registration in waiting rooms | Customers register problems online to free up phones |
| Pharmacists are trained to offer solutions to less serious ailments | Call centre staff are trained to offer solutions to less serious problems |

## POINTS TO WATCH OUT FOR

There is a danger that some participants will find reasons not to accept that anyone else has faced their problem. Somehow, they feel undermined if others have found a solution and they have not. You will hear a number of 'yes, but . . .' arguments. Help to set the scene at the outset by making participants feel good about the work they currently do and valued as members of the problem-solving team. Stress that it is their experience in this field that has made them the ideal candidates to help solve the problem.

## TOOL 32  HOW-HOW?

### WHAT THE TOOL IS

By asking how something happened, then drilling deeper each time with another 'how?', you can quickly get to the root causes of a problem, regardless of the complexity of the circumstances. By asking how something could happen, you can start to generate new ways of working.

There are many benefits to this simple but powerful technique:

■ It allows those participating to follow several parallel streams of thought, using each question and answer to stimulate further questions and answers.

■ It allows participants *not* to follow certain streams of thought – in discussion-based problem solving they would be forced to move in the same direction as everyone else.

■ It engages several senses – seeing, hearing and feeling (through the physical placement of the cards) and works in the way the brain works naturally, by making connections rather than through linear processing.

■ It allows people to change their minds and amend what they have produced as part of the process, rather than as a tacit admission of flawed thinking, which may result from more traditional processes.

### WHEN TO USE IT

■ When trying to analyse the root causes of a problem.

■ When generating new processes or working methods.

### WHAT YOU WILL NEED

■ Index cards or sticky notes.

■ A table.

### HOW TO USE IT

In the examples below, we are concentrating on generating new ideas. The same principles apply in analysing how something has gone wrong. Instead of asking, 'How could we do this?', ask, 'How did this happen?'

1 State the problem clearly and ensure that everyone understands it. Express the problem as a need, e.g. 'We need to increase our widget sales by 50 per cent in the next three months' or 'We need to attract more people to our library services to avoid library closures'.

2 Write the problem on a card.

3 Place the card to the left centre of the table.

4 Ask the group (or yourself if working alone) 'How can this be done?'

5   Write each possible answer on a separate card and place the answer cards in a column to the right of the problem card.

6   For each answer, ask again, 'How can this be done?' and write the new answers, one per card. Place each answer to the right of the card that prompted the question, so building up a hierarchy or tree.

7   Continue the process until you have solutions and no further questions.

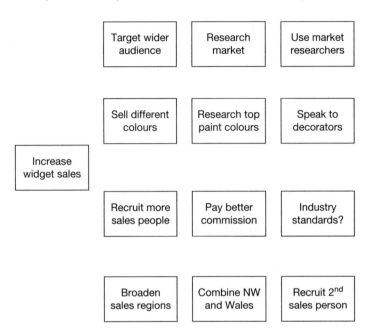

## VARIANTS
Use sticky notes on a wall/flipchart instead of cards on a table.

## POINTS TO WATCH OUT FOR
Be sensitive in facilitating this technique. Some participants may become very defensive about a failed process. Equally, they may be reluctant to discuss new ways of working that take them out of their comfort zone.

## TOOL 33 THE 5 WHYS/QUESTION EVERYTHING

### WHAT THE TOOL IS

The 5 Whys was developed as a root cause analysis technique in the 1930s by the founder of Toyota Industries, Sakichi Toyoda. Where it is suspected that there are multiple root causes, asking 'Why?' repeatedly can uncover those causes. Whether or not the 5 Whys needs to be implemented formally, simply questioning everything relating to an intractable problem – almost as a stream of consciousness exercise – can uncover hitherto unseen root causes and related issues.

5 Whys is also used as a tool at the Analyse phase of the process improvement methodology Six Sigma. The technique is best used by those who work day by day with the process that is being examined.

### WHEN TO USE IT

- When a process is not working.
- When something has gone wrong despite the process in place.
- For quality improvement.
- To determine the relationship between different causes of a problem.

### WHAT YOU WILL NEED

- A flipchart and marker pens.

### HOW TO USE IT

1  State what has gone wrong and ask why it has gone wrong.
2  Write down the answer. Answer in terms of what actually happened rather than a supposition about what might have happened. Does this get to the root cause of the problem? If so, suggest a counter-measure to prevent the recurrence of the problem.
3  If not, ask 'Why?' again and repeat step 2.

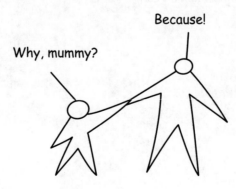

**4** Continue, repeating steps 1 and 2, until you have an answer and can go no further with the questioning.

The *5 Whys* suggests *counter-measures* rather than solutions, because a counter-measure prevents the problem recurring, where a solution may fix the presenting problem and recur when the same situation occurs again. It does not matter whether you ask 'Why?' once or 50 times – the number 5 is notional. In practice, you need to keeping ask it until you have reached the root cause.

For example:

*Why did we lose one of our major customers, ABC Corporation?*

*Because we delivered three recent shipments late.*

*Why did we deliver three recent shipments late?*

*Because we had logged incorrect shipment dates in our tracking system.*

*Why did we log incorrect shipment dates in our new tracking system?*

*Because our administrator did not know how to use the new tracking system.*

*Why did our administrator not know how to use the new tracking system?*

*Because he had received no training in its use.*

*Why did he receive no training in its use?*

*Because training on the new system was not available until this week, after the shipments had been made.*

*Solution:* Ensure that everyone is trained on the new system before using it to plan real shipments.

## POINTS TO WATCH OUT FOR

Ensure that you ask the right questions. Often, we fail to resolve a problem because we focus on the wrong aspects of it and so ask the wrong questions. For example, many organisations ask, 'Why are people not buying from us?' when a better starting question might be, 'Why are some people buying from us?' The second question allows you to focus on strengths on which you can build rather than a comprehensive investigation into your competitors' practices. You get what you focus on and some forethought about the best starting question will yield quick rewards.

## TOOL 34  THE JELLY BABY TREE

### WHAT THE TOOL IS

The Jelly Baby Tree is a public domain cartoon image of a number of 'jelly babies' in different positions and poses in a tree. It can be used in a variety of contexts, including conflict management, career advice and decisions about career prospects, organisational design and change. The power of the tool lies in both its simplicity and its ability to draw people away from emotive arguments to a rational discussion about a problem.

### WHEN TO USE IT

The Jelly Baby Tree has multiple uses, limited only by your imagination! They include:

- resolving a dispute between two colleagues.
- helping to plan an individual's career progression.
- helping to plan organisational career paths.
- organisational design.

### WHAT YOU WILL NEED

- Printed copies of the Jelly Baby Tree.
- Coloured pencils or crayons.

### HOW TO USE IT

RESOLVING A DISPUTE BETWEEN TWO COLLEAGUES

1   Bring together the two people in conflict and explain how important it is that they work together harmoniously.
2   Tell them that you want to try to experiment – that it may look odd at first, but you believe that it will help them to resolve their dispute.
3   Give each a copy of the Jelly Baby Tree and some coloured pencils.
4   Ask each of them to colour in the jelly baby that represents them and, in a different colour, the jelly baby that represents the other person.
5   Ask them to show each other their pictures and invite each, in turn, to explain why they have coloured in their chosen jelly babies.

6  Because they spend much of their time focusing on the picture and describing, almost dispassionately, why they have chosen certain jelly babies, they tend to have a calmer, more rational discussion about the reason for their conflict. Each will interpret the same character in the tree in different ways and you will hear them say, 'I chose this one because it is doing X' and the other may reply: 'Oh, I hadn't looked at it that way – I saw this character doing Y'. The Jelly Baby Tree helps them to discuss their issues as though they relate to a third party and, as the raw emotion is taken out of the discussion, so they begin to realise that they can talk reasonably to each other, that perhaps they have simply seen things from a different perspective and that there may be some room for agreement or settlement of their dispute.

HELPING TO PLAN AN INDIVIDUAL'S CAREER PROGRESSION

This should be done on a one-to-one basis because it asks someone to open up and speak quite personally:

1  Give the individual a Jelly Baby Tree and some coloured pens.

2  Ask them to study the picture and then use one colour to shade in a jelly baby that represents where they see themselves now and another colour to shade the one that represents where they would like to be in, say, a year from now or five years from now (pick the time as appropriate to the individual, possibly selecting a number of different jelly babies for different time periods).

3  Ask them to describe why they have chosen each jelly baby and how they interpret each picture. Avoid judgement or comment – do not tell them that this is not how you had viewed a particular character – it is their interpretation that counts here.

4  Ask them what they believe they would have to do to achieve the position indicated by their chosen jelly baby. Use this as the start of objective setting or their personal development planning.

HELPING TO PLAN ORGANISATIONAL CAREER PATHS AND ORGANISATIONAL DESIGN

The idea is to stimulate thinking about the current organisation and visualise the future structure using the jelly babies as symbolic of whole teams or departments:

1  Distribute copies of the Jelly Baby Tree to your fellow problem solvers and ask them to identify the various organisational teams or departments as they see them by colouring in the appropriate jelly babies.

2  Ask them to consider what they believe is working in this structure and what can be improved.

3  Let them be creative in using the Jelly Baby Tree, drawing, for example, arrows indicating where departments should be combined and other symbols to show what is working well, what should change, etc.

There are many possible uses of the Jelly Baby Tree – be creative!

## POINTS TO WATCH OUT FOR

Occasionally, people will insist that a jelly baby's pose can be interpreted in only one way and struggle to see others' interpretations of it. Stress from the outset that one of the powers of the tool is the variety of possible interpretations. For example, some see the jelly baby at the top of the tree as the high achiever who has reached the pinnacle of ambition or career progression. Others see this as someone supremely arrogant, looking down scornfully at others. Some see the jelly baby creating the tree house as an empire builder; others as someone who accepts that they are going no further in their career and are bedding in or preparing to coast along to retirement in the same role.

## TOOL 35 FUTURE SHOCK

### WHAT THE TOOL IS

This is a simple, structured method of answering the question: 'If I/we continue to do X, what will be the result N weeks/months/years from now?'

We live in a world of constant change. The world is not designed to support your organisation; instead, your organisation must adapt to the world. Ignoring external and internal factors that may have an effect on your organisation could be disastrous. *Future shock* forces you to consider the medium- to long-term effects of decisions or changes or the impact of continuing as you are without any change.

### WHEN TO USE IT

- For strategic or operational planning.

### WHAT YOU WILL NEED

- A flipchart and marker pens.

### HOW TO USE IT

1 Determine the area of your organisation that you will focus on.
2 Brainstorm the current processes and systems in use in this area.
3 Outline the results that you currently achieve in this area.
4 Now ask, for each process and system: If we continue to do this, what will the results be at some pre-specified time in the future?
5 List the suggestions as quickly as they are made, without evaluation at first.
6 Then discuss each in turn, with emphasis on what we can/will/must do to sustain or improve our current position.
7 Take care to explore the ripple effects of proposed changes on other areas of operation or likely results.

### POINTS TO WATCH OUT FOR

Some participants may feel very threatened by this approach for a number of reasons. First, those with a personal agenda may see proposed changes turning that agenda on its head; second, some may be uncomfortable at the implied threat of danger to their organisation (and thus to their jobs) should nothing change; third, some may be unhappy about the change to their own role, which will, inevitably, result if you were to make the necessary changes to the organisation. Handle it carefully and sensitively.

## TOOL 36  WHAT IF?

### WHAT THE TOOL IS

This technique was inspired by a TEDx talk from the guitarist/comedian Mike Rayburn, who adopts a 'What if?' mindset in discovering new possibilities in both stand-up comedy and music. Rayburn has suggested that, rather than starting with what is possible, we should start with what is 'cool'! If you suspend any thoughts of what you believe to be possible now, what kind of future could you create by playing 'What if'? The technique can turn apparent problems into opportunities, or produce the seed of a new idea that can be developed and grown using other techniques in this book.

### WHEN TO USE IT

- This is particularly useful in a dynamic, enterprising organisation or team that wants to explore possibilities for improvement.

### WHAT YOU WILL NEED

- A flipchart and marker pens.

### HOW TO USE IT

1   State your business issue. It may be in the form of a business problem, an explanation of a current process or a way of doing something within the organisation.
2   Participants play 'What if?' – calling out ideas of what might be possible. It does not matter how outlandish or far-fetched the ideas seem to be at first sight.
3   Record the ideas without debate, judgement or discussion.
4   You may ask the participants to rank the raw ideas before developing them further. Use other techniques, such as PMI **(see Tool 4),** to develop the ideas.

### POINTS TO WATCH OUT FOR

This technique requires participants to suspend their disbelief. It works best with a group who are open to new possibilities and excited at the thought of creative thinking around change. Encourage participants from the outset to enter into the activity with a completely open mind, alert to possibilities and freed from any perceived constraints. The essence of the technique is to think about what you *can* do, not what you cannot do. Even if you do not yet know how to do something, if it is beneficial or attractive you will find some way to make it real.

## TOOL 37   WHAT IF WE DIDN'T?

### WHAT THE TOOL IS

This is a technique for testing the validity of a solution by determining whether the benefits of not implementing it outweigh those of implementing it. **(See also *Cartesian Logic*, Tool 7, for a broader perspective.)**

### WHEN TO USE IT

■ When you have a potential solution to a problem but are unsure that it will reap the desired benefits.

### WHAT YOU WILL NEED

■ A flipchart and marker pens or paper and pens, according to the number of participants.

### HOW TO USE IT

1   State the problem and your proposed solution.

2   Brainstorm (and write down) each potential benefit of implementing the solution.

3   For each benefit, ask 'What if we didn't do/didn't need this?' and ask, for example, 'What is the cost of solving this?' and 'What is the likely cost of not solving this?'

4   Score the total 'package' of benefits (1=low and 10=high) and then score the counter-arguments on the same scale. Which carries the higher score? If the score given to benefits that would result from solving the problem is lower than that for the counter-arguments, do not proceed to solve the problem, instead accepting that it is a given and that you can live with it.

For example:

*Should we increase our staff salaries by 5 per cent to match those of our biggest competitor?*

| Potential benefits | What if we didn't?, etc. |
|---|---|
| Greater staff retention<br>Lower recruitment costs<br>More motivated staff<br>A feeling of being equal to our competitors | ■ We are in a competitive industry with high churn rates.<br>■ Our churn levels are roughly equal to our competitors', even though they are paying more.<br>■ Because churn rates are high in our industry, we would still have to recruit in high volumes.<br>■ Money is well known to be a 'hygiene' factor not a motivator.<br>■ We have actually recruited from our competitors, because our company is seen in the marketplace as treating its staff better.<br>■ We would have more money to invest in developing the business. |
| **Score 7** | **Score 9** |

Whilst the potential benefits here look appealing (score of 7), each is counterbalanced with an argument (total score of 9) which suggests that, overall, the solution is not worth implementing.

POINTS TO WATCH OUT FOR

Participants may hold on to certain 'benefits', based more on familiarity than on rational thinking. Others may defend a benefit because it was their idea. It takes a certain cold detachment to be able to reject ideas that have known benefits because the alternative may, long term, yield better results.

## TOOL 38 REFRAMING

### WHAT THE TOOL IS

Reframing is the art of rephrasing a question from a new perspective to gain new insights. It can be used, for example, to view a problem as an opportunity or a disaster as a learning experience. It is useful for putting a positive spin on something that has been viewed as negative. Even a mediocre painting may be enhanced by a nice frame.

### WHEN TO USE IT

- To gain new insights into a problem.
- To inform decision making.
- To lift the morale after something has gone wrong at work.

### WHAT YOU WILL NEED

- A flipchart and marker pens.

### HOW TO USE IT

1 Brainstorm the most pressing concerns for your team, department or organisation.
2 State each one as a question.

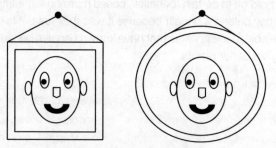

Still a vision of loveliness ...

3 For each in turn, invite participants to frame the question so that it becomes an avenue for exploration or a statement of opportunity.

For example:

| Problem | Reframe |
|---|---|
| Why aren't sufficient people buying from us? | Why do people buy from us? |
| | Who does buy from us, and can we expand that market? |
| Why is client X so difficult? | What can we do differently to work more effectively with client X? |
| | How are we being difficult with client X? |
| How can we offer the same services, faced with budget cuts? | Which services can we offer, faced with budget cuts? |
| | Which services can be made cheaper? |
| | Which services do people really need? |
| | Who else is offering a similar service? |
| | Who wants our current services? |

Now use other tools to explore the best of the reframed statements in more detail.

## POINTS TO WATCH OUT FOR

The chief enemies of this process are cynicism and scepticism. Some participants will view the process as unrealistic – trying to create something positive where there are no positives. Acknowledge their concerns at the outset to effectively 'inoculate' them against this behaviour.

## TOOL 39 THE RIPPLE EFFECT (SYSTEMS THINKING)

### WHAT THE TOOL IS

A well-designed organisation is like a machine, in which every component has an important part to play. A change to one tiny component in the machine may have severe or complex implications for another part of the machine, although the consequences may be distant in time and space from the change.

A problem solved in one part of an organisation may have ripple effects in other areas of the organisation, again sometimes appearing only some time after the solution is effected. The *ripple effect* is a technique designed to tease out the effects that a change made in one specific area of the organisation has on all the other areas of the organisation.

### WHEN TO USE IT

- When you plan a major change in your operational area and need to know if/how it affects others and, as such, whether your plan is workable in its current form.
- You may want to use the *solution effect analysis* method (**see Tool 43**) first, to satisfy yourself that you have looked at all the possible side-effects that you could predict before looking at the wider organisation.

### WHAT YOU WILL NEED

- Paper and pens.
- A flipchart and marker pens.

### HOW TO USE IT

You will need a group of people representing as many areas of the organisation as possible.

1 State the problem for which you have a possible solution.
2 Ensure that all participants understand the nature of the problem – state it as factually as possible, avoiding any emotional hooks and remembering that the participants may not understand the jargon you use in your own operational area.
3 State your proposed solution, again ensuring understanding.
4 Now ask the participants to reflect silently for five minutes on the possible ramifications for their area of work, noting down questions and concerns.

**5** After five minutes, ask participants to raise their questions and concerns.

**6** Do not worry if you do not have immediate answers to each concern, but thank them and note it.

**7** Invite participants to suggest modifications to your ideas that could reduce or remove the effect on their operational area without rendering your solution unworkable.

**8** When all suggestions have been discussed, thank the participants and agree a time by which you will report back to them.

**9** After the meeting, assimilate their ideas and rework your solution.

**10** Distribute the revised solution to the participants, inviting final comments by a specified date.

## POINTS TO WATCH OUT FOR

This method relies on the goodwill of people who may not stand to benefit at all from the solution to your problem. Indeed, it may create additional work for some of them. Take care to invite a good cross-section, and be sensitive to those who would be offended if not invited to join in. Sadly, office politics will play a part here.

Do not use this method for relatively small changes – only for those whose reach may extend beyond your own work area.

## REFERENCE

Senge, P.M. (2006) *The Fifth Discipline: The Art and Practice of the Learning Organization.* London: Random House Business.

TOOL 40 # WHAT I NEED FROM YOU

## WHAT THE TOOL IS

Rarely can we solve a work-based problem alone and rarely does a problem affect only one person or area of an organisation.

This technique is designed to tease out what each interested party needs from the others in order to ensure that the problem can be solved satisfactorily for everyone involved.

## WHEN TO USE IT

■ When you have reached a solution to a problem and want to ensure that everyone knows what may be expected of them as the solution is implemented. Ideally, use this after collaborative, cross-departmental or cross-functional problem solving.

## WHAT YOU WILL NEED

■ Flipchart paper and marker pens.

■ Reusable adhesive or tape.

■ Sticky notes.

■ Pens.

■ Camera or mobile phone with camera.

## HOW TO USE IT

1  Invite representatives of each area of the organisation who will be affected if you implement a proposed solution to a problem.

2  Write the name of each department represented on a separate flipchart sheet and fix the sheets to the walls.

3  State the original problem and your proposed solution. Invite participants to ask questions to ensure their understanding of both the problem and the solution.

4  Ask each one to reflect, in silence, on what they would need from your department/ business area and others' departments/business areas if the solution is to be viable. Each request should be written on a separate sticky note and signed by its author, then posted on the flipchart page representing the department or business area of whom the request is being made. For example, if someone representing HR needs something from IT, then they write the request and post it on the IT flipchart page. If requests are time-critical, then the time for fulfilment of the request should be added to the sticky note. If the requests can be fulfilled only by specific individuals, their names should be added to the sticky note.

5  After posting their requests, participants should walk around the room and read the requests on each flipchart page to get a broad picture of others' thoughts.

6  Finally, participants should stop at the flipchart relating to their own area of work, then in turn, in plenary, ask requestors clarifying questions to ensure that they truly understand what is being asked of them. If necessary, the written requests should be modified by those who wrote them.

7  If appropriate, additional specific requests should be added to the flipchart pages to balance any modifications made in the plenary session.

8  Photograph each flipchart page and either send the appropriate photo to each participant or type and send the appropriate requests to each participant.

There is a nice spin-off effect from this method – almost by stealth it achieves buy-in from other departments as you involve them in the process. It can be even more powerful if you involve the same participants first in the problem-solving process using one of the methods in this book, and then facilitate this process so that everyone knows exactly what is expected of them.

## POINTS TO WATCH OUT FOR

There may be a sense among the participants of 'what's in this for me?' – they may see that, whilst they are helping you, they get nothing in return. This problem is removed if those participating are also in the problem-solving or decision-making process which preceded this event.

## TOOL 41 CONCENTRATION DIAGRAMS

### WHAT THE TOOL IS

This is a visual representation, built up over some time, of *where* a problem or defect is occurring. At the centre of the diagram is, for example, a picture of a product, a machine, a process, a map of an area, a floor plan of an office or factory, and the diagram is annotated with marks indicating where a problem has occurred. This is a useful tool in ensuring that the right problem is being solved and that the focus is in the most appropriate area.

### WHEN TO USE IT

■ To discover exactly where a problem is occurring, which may, in turn, reveal patterns of occurrence of the problem.

### WHAT YOU WILL NEED

■ A flipchart and marker pens.

### HOW TO USE IT

1 Draw a map of the building, the room, the area or the system.
2 Determine whether you already have data about the location in which a problem occurs. If you do, then go to step 4.
3 If you do not have that data, list the events that you need to record to connect them to locations.
4 If recording more than one event, assign symbols to each event.
5 Map the events on the diagram.
6 Analyse patterns or trends in the diagram.

For example:

> *Our office cleaners have been complaining that there are coffee stains on the carpets and that they are struggling to keep pace with the number of people who appear to throw more coffee on the carpets than they ingest. We want to know where the worst stains are and whether we can detect a pattern that suggests why this is happening.*

First we map out the areas that the cleaners tell us are worst affected – the areas around the reception desk, guest seating area, kitchenette and photocopier room. Then we mark the worst areas of staining on the map.

From the map, it seems that there is a trail of stains between the reception desk, kitchenette and guest seating area and another cluster to the side of the photocopier. We can guess that the receptionists, eager to welcome our guests, slop coffee as they carry it from the kitchenette to the guest seating area, and that people photocopying rest their coffee cups on the side of the copier.

Although this is a trivial example, it illustrates how the concentration diagram can be used to detect patterns, useful in analysing root causes of a problem.

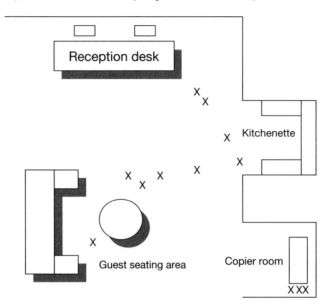

## POINTS TO WATCH OUT FOR

At first sight, the method may look trivial. Surely we would know where a problem is occurring? In reality, although we may be vaguely aware of a recurring problem, we tend to guess at the reasons. Plotting the occurrence by location gives us useful evidence to help resolve the problem. For example, does a particular problem occur only in one branch of our organisation? Does it happen in only one country and not in others? What is different about that branch or country? Having discovered patterns of occurrence, you may choose to use other tools like *The 5 Whys* **(see Tool 33)** or *How-how?* **(see Tool 32)** to explore the causes in more depth.

## REFERENCE

Andersen, B., Fagerhaug, T. and Belz, M. (2010) *Root Cause Analysis and Improvement in the Healthcare Sector: A Step-by-Step Guide.* Milwaukee, Wisconsin: ASQ Quality Press.

## TOOL 42   THE PARETO ANALYSIS – SIMPLIFIED VERSION

### WHAT THE TOOL IS

The Pareto analysis is used to ensure that the first steps you take solve the maximum number of problems or eliminate the greatest number of causes.

Italian economist Vilfredo Pareto observed that 80 per cent of Italy's wealth lay in the hands of 20 per cent of the population and vice versa. In the 1940s, management expert Joseph Juran began to adopt the ratio in other areas of business.

*Pareto's Law* (also known as the 80/20 rule) has been adopted by the business community to describe paradoxical ratios. For example, 80 per cent of the benefit from a project may come from 20 per cent of the total effort and 80 per cent of the problems encountered in a particular situation may come from 20 per cent of the causes. It was first applied in business circles in the 1940s by Romanian-born American engineer and management consultant, Joseph M. Juran. Where Pareto's Law was described as the 'vital few and the trivial many', Juran called it 'the vital few and the useful many' to deter people from dismissing the 80 per cent, which may yield important information.

The ratio may be applied to many aspects of work, and raises some interesting questions about your operations, for example:

- 80 per cent of your work yields 20 per cent of the result and vice versa. This suggests that perfection is achievable only at great cost. It may be better to release a service or product that is 80 per cent developed, based on 20 per cent of total effort, rather than try to achieve perfection, which would cost the other 80 per cent of effort.
- 20 per cent of your clients give 80 per cent of your revenue and vice versa. Are you spending a disproportionate amount of time pursuing non-profitable clients?
- 20 per cent of your sales force generates 80 per cent of your profits. Are you rewarding them adequately?
- 20 per cent of your products and services generate 80 per cent of your profits. Is it time to reduce the range of products and services and expand the market for your more profitable items?

Whilst the 80/20 ratio would not survive scientifically rigorous testing, it is a useful rule of thumb in determining how much effort we should put into a complex task.

### WHEN TO USE IT

- To determine where to focus management effort in solving a problem.

### WHAT YOU WILL NEED

- A flipchart and marker pens.
- Paper and pens.

## HOW TO USE IT

There are many variants on the Pareto diagram, and some require detailed statistical analysis. Here is a simplified version, which can be adapted to many situations to discover the primary causes of major problems and thus show you where to focus your main management efforts.

1 Identify and list your problems.

2 Identify the root cause of each problem.

3 Score the problems.

4 Cluster the problems by root cause.

5 Add the scores for each cluster.

6 Take action to resolve the problems.

For example:

*I have assumed responsibility for a team that manufactures widgets. The level of customer complaints and accompanying returned products is rising sharply. I need to understand where to focus my management effort for greatest impact.*

I list the problems I have observed in the team, the likely causes and the number of complaints. I have clustered the problems by root cause:

| Problem number | Problem | Cause (from step 2) | Score (from step 3) |
| --- | --- | --- | --- |
| 1 | Misaddressed packages | Distribution department error | 2 |
| 2 | Late delivery | Distribution department error | 4 |
| 3 | Only 40 widgets in a packet of 50 | Machine error | 9 |
| 4 | Packets not properly sealed | Machine error | 5 |
| 5 | Widget sizes vary | Operator error (poor training) | 29 |
| 6 | Widgets are discoloured | Operator error (poor training) | 19 |

Now I order the problems in descending order of complaints:

Operator error: 48

Machine error: 14

Distribution department error: 6

It is immediately obvious that the greatest source of problems comes from operator error. In a more complex scenario, it is worth charting the causes and scores to see a graphical distribution. For this example:

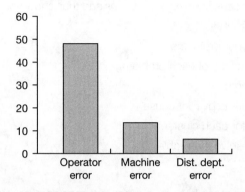

From the distribution of errors, I know that I should focus my first efforts on training the staff. After this, I may wish to have a quiet word with the maintenance department and distribution department.

## POINTS TO WATCH OUT FOR

The method is useful in identifying the most significant root causes of problems but takes no account of the cost of a solution. You may need to undertake a separate cost-benefit analysis once you are aware of the root causes.

## REFERENCE

50minutes.com (2015) *Pareto's Principle: Expand your Business!* 50Minutes.com.

## TOOL 43  THE SOLUTION EFFECT ANALYSIS

### WHAT THE TOOL IS

This technique is the reverse of a cause and effect diagram, designed to check whether a solution actually solves a problem, to compare effects of different solutions, to ensure that the chosen solution does not cause even bigger problems and to identify any other actions that may be necessary to ensure that a solution is fit for purpose.

### WHEN TO USE IT

■ Consider using in conjunction with the *Ripple effect* (**see Tool 39**). This method will help you to identify possible ramifications of your solution in your own area. The *Ripple effect* will help you to identify possible effects of your solution across the wider organisation.

### WHAT YOU WILL NEED

■ A flipchart, paper and marker pens.

### HOW TO USE IT

1  Use other methods outlined in this book to create the solution to a problem.
2  Use a fishbone diagram to identify the major effects of the solution.
3  Brainstorm possible further effects of those major effects.
4  Analyse those effects and look for solutions.
5  Amend the original solution or re-evaluate to create a new, more effective solution.

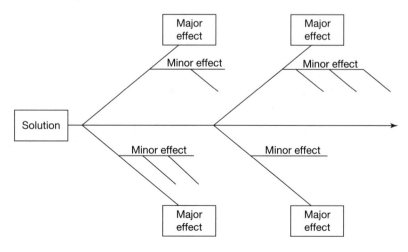

### POINTS TO WATCH OUT FOR

You will need a detailed knowledge of your organisation or a range of participants from across the organisation to help you in the process.

## TOOL 44 THE WORK MAP

### WHAT THE TOOL IS

The *Work map* can be used by individuals or teams working together to recoup time – the most valuable commodity at work. It produces a graphical snapshot of the individual's or group's work and prompts a series of questions about how time is being used, where a disproportionate amount of time may be used in undeserving areas, what we want from others and they from us and how we can start to rationalise what we do and so start to use our time more effectively.

### WHEN TO USE IT

- The work map is very useful in analysing where your own time goes and discovering ways of recouping lost time.
- It can also be a powerful tool to use with a small team working together.

### WHAT YOU WILL NEED

- Pen and paper.

### HOW TO USE IT

1 On a piece of paper (at least A4 in size) and turned to landscape, draw a small circle in the centre and put your name in the circle.
2 Consider all the people or groups of people both inside and outside work who require something from you or have expectations of something at work – it may be that you deliver goods, services, reports, information to them – it does not matter what you offer, as long as they have some expectation that you will deliver something to them. These groups and individuals might include, for example, your boss, your direct reports, key customers or clients and others. Ranged around the central circle, draw another circle for each person or group who requires something from you and put their name inside the circle that represents them. Note that if several people or groups require exactly the same thing from you, their names can be entered in the same circle. If there are differences in their expectations of you, no matter how subtle, draw a separate circle for each one.

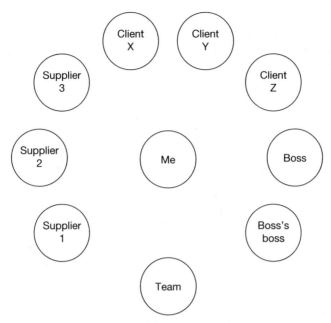

3   Connect each circle to the centre circle with lines like spokes of a bicycle wheel. Above each connecting line, write a very brief description of what you believe each of these 'stakeholders' requires from you.

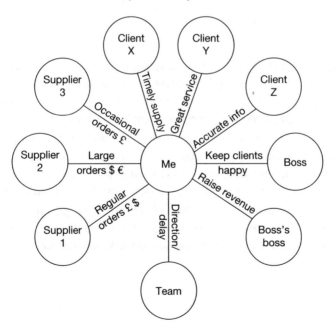

4   Consider how each stakeholder would evaluate your offerings to them. Do they
    measure it in terms of quantity, quality, cost or time, or a combination of these?
    By each circle, indicate how they evaluate it using *Qn* (quantity), *Ql* (quality), *C*
    (cost), *T* (time).

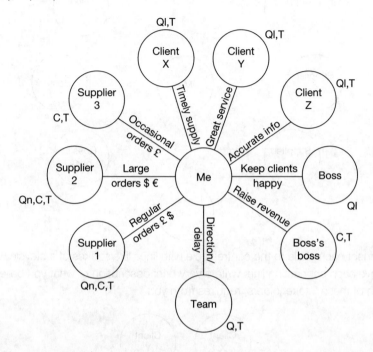

5   From each stakeholder circle, draw a line and write on this line what each
    stakeholder does with whatever you offer them. For example, if you send
    stakeholder X a monthly report, what do they do with the information in that
    report? **(See completed work map overleaf.)**

6   Now go back to the lines connecting each stakeholder to the central circle. If
    you believe that what you wrote above the line represents what the stakeholder
    expects from you, now write below the line what you need or expect from the
    stakeholder in order to provide this. **(See completed work map overleaf.)**

7   Finally, consider where you spend the bulk of your working time. Shade in the
    circles representing the stakeholders who, whether rightly or wrongly, take up
    most of your working time. **(See completed work map below.)**

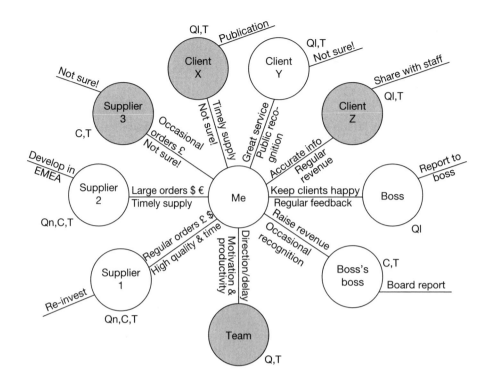

Now you have a picture of your working life, which may prompt a series of questions:

1   How do you know what each stakeholder wants from you? When did you last discuss it with them?

2   How do you know how they evaluate what you do for them? When did you last discuss it with them?

3   Do they know exactly what you expect/need from them in order to meet their expectations? When did you last discuss it with them?

4   How do you know how they use whatever you deliver to them? When did you last discuss it with them?

5   If you are spending a disproportionate amount of working time with certain stakeholders, are you neglecting others who would value spending more time with you?

Notice in the example diagram, some of the expectations are marked as 'Not sure' as the end results of whatever I am providing to the stakeholders. If I am not sure what they do with whatever I provide, then I must go and speak to those stakeholders and re-establish what we need from each other and why we are doing what we are doing.

The idea is to question everything. You may discover, for example, that you produce a detailed report for one stakeholder who needs only a high-level, bulleted summary. You may discover that you are taking too much time to produce something of quality when the stakeholder requires something basic, or perhaps requires nothing at all and simply has not told you (because you did not ask).

Go back and talk to the people you have included in your diagram and discuss mutual expectations. You will be surprised at how much extra time you can gain from reducing some of the work you do for them and, in some cases, stopping it altogether.

## POINTS TO WATCH OUT FOR

Be careful not to defend something that you have always done, simply because you have always done it. It is important in using the work map to be realistic and to be willing to let go of things that no longer work. It may also take some courage to go and have the necessary conversations with people about your mutual expectations, but the rewards will far outweigh the discomfort.

# THE COMPETING VALUES FRAMEWORK

## WHAT THE TOOL IS

Kim Cameron and Robert Quinn are regarded as the world's experts on corporate culture and, as a result of extensive research, produced a diagnostic tool that helps to analyse and, ultimately, change corporate culture. A spin-off effect, not documented in their classic book **(see the Reference section at the end of this tool)** is that their model provides a wonderful tool for making career decisions. It is in that light that it is included here. If you are debating whether or not to apply to a particular organisation for a job, then this tool will help you to frame your findings so that you can test whether the organisation is for you.

## WHEN TO USE IT

- When you are looking for a new job and choosing the organisations for which you could work comfortably or (if seeking a challenge) change!

## WHAT YOU WILL NEED

- Pen and paper.

## HOW TO USE IT

Cameron and Quinn's extensive research into organisational culture suggested that every organisation, regardless of whether it is in the public, private or third sector (voluntary, social enterprise, charity), displays a combination of characteristics in four particular areas, which they named as:

| Clan | Adhocracy |
|------|-----------|
| Hierarchy | Market |

They recently added a second descriptor to each area:

| Clan | Adhocracy |
|------|-----------|
| (Collaborate) | (Create) |
| Hierarchy | Market |
| (Control) | (Compete) |

Any two boxes that are diagonally opposite each other are considered to be diametrically opposed. For example, the greater the *clan* characteristics displayed by an organisation, the fewer *market* characteristics it will display and vice versa.

Cameron and Quinn described the cultural characteristics typical in each area and, as you begin to understand them, so you can start to choose the type of organisation in which you would feel comfortable working. Broadly, the characteristics are as follows:

| Clan (Collaborate) | Adhocracy (Create) |
|---|---|
| Friendly and sharing family | Dynamic and entrepreneurial |
| Leaders are 'parents' or mentors | Leaders are innovative and risk takers |
| Loyalty and tradition | Experimental and inventive |
| High commitment | Leading edge |
| Emphasis on personal development | Emphasis on growth and new resources |
| Sensitivity to internal and external clients | Success is new services or products |
| Participation and consensus | Individual initiative and freedom |
| **Hierarchy (Control)** | **Market (Compete)** |
| Formal, structured and procedural | Results-oriented, getting the job done |
| Leaders are efficient organisers | Competitive and goal-driven |
| Smooth running is essential | Leaders are tough and demanding |
| Formal rules and policies | Emphasis on winning |
| Stable and dependable service | Achievement of measurable goals |
| Secure employment | Success is in market share and penetration |

In purely personal terms, a strong preference or dislike for a particular quadrant is likely to indicate the following:

| Quadrant | Like/want it because . . . | Dislike/do not want it because . . . |
|---|---|---|
| **Clan** | You like to feel valued<br>You like to work collaboratively | You would feel suffocated<br>You do not always want to work closely with others or as part of a team |
| **Hierarchy** | You like the sense of security that comes from rules and process | You would feel constrained by rules and process |
| **Market** | You like to work under pressure<br>You like to meet targets | You would feel too pressurised<br>You would feel there is too much emphasis on achievement of goals |
| **Adhocracy** | You like the sense of freedom<br>You like to be a soloist | You would feel that things are out of control<br>You would miss working in a team |

Now imagine a scale of 0 to 50 for each quadrant, starting at the centre of the box and radiating out towards the corners. Score each quadrant based on its appeal to you and join the dots.

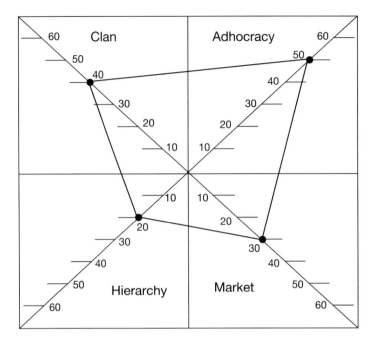

In this hypothetical example, I want a medium high clan score and a high adhocracy score. I want a low hierarchy score and a medium market score. At a personal level, it suggests that I do not much like being constrained by rules but enjoy the freedom to think and act for myself; I am a reasonable, but not strong, team player; I am moderately driven by targets but do not like too much pressure.

Now try to discover as much as you can about the company that you are thinking of joining and overlay on top of your diagram a picture of how you see that company using a different style or different coloured pen. You might like to add a key to indicate which is your score and which relates to the company. How would you score them in each area? How close is your ideal to what you perceive as the actuality of the company? Where are the gaps? Can you tolerate them? Would you be applying for a sufficiently senior position to be able to change anything?

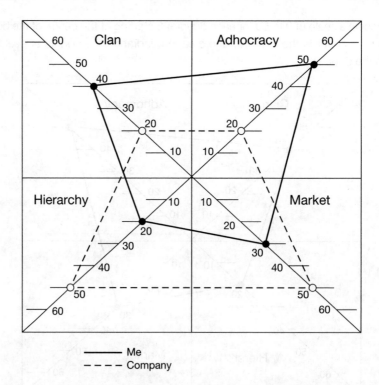

If there is a close match, then the company looks like a good choice for you. If there are discrepancies, then you need to think carefully about whether it is for you. Look at the following points for guidance.

### POINTS TO WATCH OUT FOR

Perhaps the biggest difficulty is in finding out what an organisation is really like. After all, six organisations working in the same area will claim, on their websites, to be the best in their field, which means that five of them are deluded or not telling the truth! Look at press reports, talk to people who already work for the organisation and do the most comprehensive research you can to find out what it is really like to work there. Then bear in mind that you have a choice:

- If the culture of an organisation does not match your needs, are you prepared to tolerate it and grin and bear the attendant frustrations?

- If the culture of an organisation does not match your needs, are you applying for a job at a sufficiently senior level to be able to change some aspects of that culture and so make it more tolerable?

- If a particular organisation has to have a certain culture to support its work and you are unhappy with that culture, are you sure that you are working in a field that really suits you?

■ To what extent do external forces, such as regulatory or compliance requirements, shape an organisational culture? For example, pharmaceutical companies are profit-driven and heavily regulated. It may be that a research and development department maintains a sub-culture of *adhocracy* but, inevitably, their two biggest cultural footprints will be in *hierarchy* and *market*. The Armed Services are an interesting mix – at regimental level they show strong *clan* characteristics; at HQ level, *hierarchy;* in field operations, *adhocracy;* and, possibly, at recruitment level, *market.*

## REFERENCE
Cameron, K.S. and Quinn, R.E. (2011) *Diagnosing and Changing Organizational Culture Using the Competing Values Framework.* San Francisco: John Wiley & Sons.

## TOOL 46 TIMELINING

### WHAT THE TOOL IS

A very powerful group technique, much of which is conducted in silence, to ascertain where the group should focus its efforts, what it can realistically hope to achieve and by when, and the likely level of involvement of individuals within the group.

### WHEN TO USE IT

■ When a group needs to plan and prioritise its actions.

### WHAT YOU WILL NEED

■ Flipchart paper and marker pens.
■ Sticky notes.
■ A room with plenty of space for participants to walk around.

### HOW TO USE IT

ROUND 1 – MAJOR ACHIEVEMENTS

1 Around a room, post flipchart sheets, each headed with a date – the first shows the date six months from now, the second a year from now, the third eighteen months from now, the fourth two years from now – as far ahead as you believe you can look or need to plan.

2 Ask participants to walk around the flipchart sheets, in complete silence, staring at each date and imagining what they could achieve/must achieve/would like to achieve (as appropriate) by then, then walk to the next and the next in sequence until they cannot imagine their work any further into the future.

3 When they reach the latest date at which they can visualise something being achieved, they should write on the flipchart sheet a brief description of the milestone they intend to reach by this stage.

4 Participants then walk back in the opposite direction, writing on each flipchart sheet the major achievement(s) they expect by each date in turn. Remember that this is all done in silence.

ROUND 2 – MILESTONES

1 Participants walk to the flipchart displaying the furthest date (in the future) at which they had marked a milestone achievement.

2 Then they consider what has to happen at earlier dates to make the end date feasible.

3  They walk back and write on each flipchart in turn the major phases that must be finished at each specific date in order to achieve their end goal. Again, this is done in silence.

### ROUND 3 – ACTIONS

1  Give participants sticky notes.

2  Ask them to walk round the flipcharts, noting on separate sticky notes the actions that have to be taken to achieve the milestones. They should write one action per sticky note and stick them on the appropriately dated flipchart sheets.

### ROUND 4 – PEOPLE

1  Finally, the participants are allowed to speak! Participants should consider who must undertake each of the actions in round 3.

2  They should seek out the appropriate people (if they are in the room and participating) and take them to the appropriate flipchart sheets, ask them to undertake the work in question and, with their agreement, assign the actions to them by putting their names or initials on the appropriate sticky notes.

### ROUND 5 – ASSIMILATION

1  Everyone now walks through the flipchart sheets from earliest to latest date, reading the milestones, actions, assigned names and ultimate achievements and double-checks the feasibilities and dependencies, asking permission from others to make changes, as appropriate.

2  Take photographs of each flipchart sheets in sequence and have them typed up as a high-level action plan, to be discussed (if necessary) in more detail at a later team meeting.

## POINTS TO WATCH OUT FOR

Some people struggle with silence, and yet it is the silence that gives power to this method. Explain at the outset the need for silence in the early stages, with the promise of conversation later!

Some participants will be over-ambitious, believing that they can achieve more than is feasible in the time available. Ensure that, in round 4, participants check carefully the likelihood of achieving the actions, milestones and ultimate goals by the allocated date. Ask them to check dependencies extremely carefully, asking themselves (and each other) what must have happened before this can start. In a loosely structured way, they are creating a critical path analysis.

## REFERENCE

The provenance of this method is unknown. I am indebted to Angela Peacock and Jeremy Lewis of the People Development Team (www.pdtglobal.com) for showing me the technique and demonstrating it so powerfully with clients.

## TOOL 47　ONE QUESTION

### WHAT THE TOOL IS
This is a simple, yet effective, approach to help a group to ask the right question in order to solve a problem, then explore sub-questions.

### WHEN TO USE IT
- When attempts to solve a problem have failed or solutions have not been forthcoming, it is often because the wrong question is being asked, or the problem is badly framed. *One question* can help the participants to reframe a problem as a question so that it is easier to find a viable solution.

### WHAT YOU WILL NEED
- Flipchart paper and marker pens.
- Sticky coloured dots.
- Sticky notes.

### HOW TO USE IT

1 Outline the problem in the broadest terms, answering participants' questions to ensure that everyone understands it fully.

2 Each participant then frames the single question that they believe needs to be answered first to start to create a solution. Participants write their questions on sticky notes and post them on a wall or a flipchart.

3 Read out each question in turn and ask participants to vote for the question that best encapsulates the problem to be solved. You may choose to vote by a show of hands or by placement of sticky coloured dots. Participants may vote for any question except their own.

4 When everyone has voted, read out the question that gained the majority of the votes.

5 Ask the group whether it needs to be refined in light of the other questions – is there anything missing that would make solution finding easier?

6 Now you have the final question, use other methods outlined in this book to resolve it.

7 It may be that reading out all the questions suggests that there are sub-questions or sub-topics to be explored. Discuss with the group which other questions are worth exploring, or use the voting system to pick up, say, the second and third most popular questions as voted by the participants and explore those, too.

## POINTS TO WATCH OUT FOR

It is sometimes more effective at step 7 to pick up sub-questions by the number of votes they have received, rather than by discussing them with the group. Often, a more senior or dominant person may try to sway the group towards their question, and the voting process removes this possibility.

## TOOL 48 PEER ASSIST

### WHAT THE TOOL IS

*Peer assist* is a variant of *Action learning* **(see Tool 49),** bringing together peers to give feedback on an issue, problem, idea, project, etc. The principle behind it is that, whatever you are about to do, someone has probably done it before you and you can benefit from their experience. It works best with a group of six to eight people.

### WHEN TO USE IT

- When you are starting a new project and could benefit from the advice of more experienced people.
- When you are facing a problem that others have faced in the past.
- When you are planning a project similar to one that another group has been involved in or even completed.

### WHAT YOU WILL NEED

- Working space and time.

### HOW TO USE IT

Before the peer assist session:

1 Determine who has experience of the topic to be discussed.
2 Email them to present your purpose and plan for the session.
3 Set a date for the session.

During the session:

1 The facilitator introduces the session, the people and the roles people will play.
2 The person wanting help presents their case. Participants speak only to clarify their understanding at this stage.
3 Facilitated discussion.
4 Check any actions or agreements with the group and presenter.
5 Close.

### VARIANTS

If a number of people are involved in a new project and seek assistance, you may choose to divide the large group into smaller, more manageable groups and have parallel discussions with one presenter and one facilitator per smaller group. Follow the format above but add in a plenary session between steps 4 and 5 in which the whole group convenes for a plenary sharing of information and ideas.

## POINTS TO WATCH OUT FOR

Plan ahead for a *Peer assist* session. If you leave it too late, you will have no chance to implement the ideas that come from it.

## REFERENCE

There are many articles online about peer-assisted learning, but most of the books focus on classroom methods in school.

 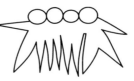

## TOOL 49 ACTION LEARNING

### WHAT THE TOOL IS

*Action learning* was the brainchild of Professor Reg Revans, the Director of Education for the British National Coal Board. Revans believed that peer groups and team members are the best coaches and facilitators for problem solving, although acknowledged that if a team (a 'set' in action learning parlance) lacks the ability to be reflective – a key component of action learning, has difficult team members or needs help with processes or direction, an outside facilitator can assist in the process. Action learning sets help solve problems rather than recommend actions.

### WHEN TO USE IT

■ This is useful after more formal training to keep a peer group together so that they continue to learn and assist each other in problem solving, decision making and learning.

### WHAT YOU WILL NEED

■ Working space and time.

### HOW TO USE IT

1 Establish a relatively small, mutually supportive group of four to eight people, ideally peers from a number of departments.
2 State clearly the organisational problem (or opportunity to be developed).
3 Group members ask clarifying questions.
4 Group members now focus on asking the right questions to help the presenter to learn, rather than on finding solutions, exploring both what is known and what is not yet known and using questions to break away from received wisdom about the past and 'how we do things around here'. Good open-ended questions, asked one at a time, rather than 'stacked' work best.
5 Members are encouraged to be challenging in their questioning to help the presenter to see an issue from other perspectives whilst remaining supportive and attentive to the presenter's feelings. They must not give personal solutions or work from their own, personal agendas. Examples of good questions are:
   ■ 'Could you say a little more about that?'
   ■ 'Are you saying that . . . ?'
   ■ 'What happened after that?'
   ■ 'Have you considered exploring X?'

And, towards the end of the discussion:

- 'Is there anything we have not covered?'
- 'Are there any aspects that you would like to explore further?'

6   Members are now asked to reflect upon the questions.

7   After this phase of questioning and reflection, action items are identified.

## POINTS TO WATCH OUT FOR
The facilitator must ensure that:

- the presenter never feels attacked;
- only one person speaks at a time;
- the presenter is given time to reflect on the questions and space to answer them;
- that the group members ask questions rather than give advice;
- that no group member tries to control the direction of the discussion.

## REFERENCES
Butler, L. and Leach, N. (2011) *Action Learning for Change: A Practical Guide for Managers.* Oxford: Management Books 2000 Ltd.

Pedler, M. (2013) *Facilitating Action Learning: A Practitioner's Guide.* Maidenhead: Open University Press.

# STORY CIRCLES

## WHAT THE TOOL IS

Many collaborative techniques involve opinion, judgement and subjective viewpoints. Whilst they draw on the experience of the participants, they do not necessarily invite participants to share their experience directly. *Story circles* use participants' real-life stories to add flesh to the bones of an idea.

## WHEN TO USE IT

- To elicit the experiences of a group of people who have already done something in an area in which you are just becoming involved.
- To test the viability of an idea before implementing it.
- To understand better how to implement a particular change at work.

## WHAT YOU WILL NEED

- A presenter or small group of presenters with something to learn.
- A group of (maximum eight) people with practical experience in the area to be discussed and the generosity of spirit to help someone less experienced.

## HOW TO USE IT

1 The presenter discusses an idea, a challenge, a topic in which he/she is seeking help.

2 The facilitator asks a number of open questions, designed to elicit experience in the area of discussion and allows sufficient time for participants to tell their stories, which illustrate their personal experiences of the issue.

3 The presenter may also question participants to get them to delve deeper into their stories.

## POINTS TO WATCH OUT FOR

The *Story circle* needs strong facilitation to ensure that participants simply tell their stories, rather than offer their experiences as best practice. Often, the disaster story can be more useful in illustrating points to watch and areas of danger.

Ensure that no single participant dominates the session in an effort to prove that they have more experience than others – the power of the method comes from the variety of experiences offered.

# TOOL 51 | SWIM LANE DIAGRAMS (RUMMLER-BRACHE DIAGRAMS)

## WHAT THE TOOL IS

Swim lane (aka swimlane) diagrams were created by Geary Rummler and Alan Brache to clarify interconnections between teams, departments and processes and, as a result, to determine the efficiency of the processes. The diagrams are called swim lanes because of the horizontal rows used, which look like the lane markers in a swimming pool. Sometimes, they are referred to as cross-functional flowcharts.

## WHEN TO USE IT

- Use it to test the efficiency of a process that involves a number of participants in different functional areas.

## WHAT YOU WILL NEED

- Pen and paper.

## HOW TO USE IT

1 Select the business process to be analysed.
2 State the specific process that you are working on.
3 Identify each participant in the process that you are analysing.
4 List each participant in the left column of the diagram. Each participant is given a horizontal row (swim lane).
5 List the steps in the process as it is currently executed.
6 Map each step to the participant who executes it.
7 Analyse the diagram and assess whether any part of the process can be improved. For example:
   - Are there any missing steps?
   - Is there any duplication of effort?
   - Is there any step that adds no value?

Here is a fragment from a warehouse process:

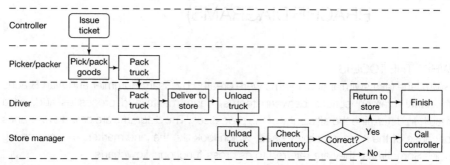

In our example, you can see that both picker/packer and driver load the truck, which reduces the number of people in the warehouse picking and packing. The driver and the store manager unload the truck together. This may be a useful way of double-checking the inventory, but it may be inefficient.

Having analysed the diagram, you may choose to draw another swim lane diagram to show how the process could/should work. This may result in, for example, the removal or addition of steps, removal or addition of participants in the process or combination of steps.

## VARIANTS
You may want to start by creating a swim lane diagram for the highest-level processes and then create new diagrams to explore one or more sub-processes in additional detail.

## POINTS TO WATCH OUT FOR
Be careful not to eliminate steps whose purpose is not immediately obvious – there may be good reasons why those steps exist and need to be perpetuated. Equally, do not maintain a step for fear of hurting someone's feelings by removing it – retain only the steps that serve a real purpose.

## REFERENCE
Damelio, R. (2011) *The Basics of Process Mapping.* New York: Productivity Press.

PART 4

# LARGE GROUP PROBLEM-SOLVING TECHNIQUES

TOOL 52 CRAWFORD'S SLIP

## WHAT THE TOOL IS

Crawford's slip was originated by a Dr C.C. Crawford of the University of Southern California in the 1920s and so named, perhaps rather unimaginatively, because participants write their ideas on slips of paper.

## WHEN TO USE IT

- When time is limited and you need a lot of ideas but have little time for discussion.
- When people are reluctant to speak out in front of the group.

The method works particularly well in cultures or organisations where people are reserved and prefer to contribute anonymously.

## WHAT YOU WILL NEED

- Paper (or sticky notes) and pens.

## HOW TO USE IT

1 Distribute slips of paper or sticky notes to each participant.
2 Ask them to write ideas on the topic being discussed, one idea per slip. Contributions are made anonymously.
3 You may offer to summarise the responses after the event (which encourages participation).
4 Collect the slips when you see that participants are running out of ideas.
5 Outside the event, collate and sort the answers by subtopic or theme.
6 After the event, send a summary of ideas with a thank you email to participants.

## POINTS TO WATCH OUT FOR

The method can be frustrating for those who prefer more active discussion and for those who have few ideas and become bored with the process as they wait for others to finish writing their ideas.

## REFERENCE

Dettmer, H.W. (2003) *Brainpower Networking Using the Crawford Slip Method.* Bloomington: Trafford.

## TOOL 53 THE CHARRETTE PROCEDURE

### WHAT THE TOOL IS

Several small groups brainstorm solutions to a problem, facilitated by 'recorders' who, at a given time signal, move to new groups to continue the process there. After several iterations, recorders pool and present their ideas.

The word *charrette* is French for cart. Allegedly, a cart would come to collect the scale models produced by architecture students at the École des Beaux-Arts in Paris in the nineteenth century. The students, working hard at the last minute so that they did not miss the deadline as the cart arrived, were said to be working *en charrette*.

### WHEN TO USE IT

- For strategic planning.
- For organisational design.
- For discussion of issues/problems/decisions that cut across departmental boundaries.

### WHAT YOU WILL NEED

- A large workspace.
- Flipcharts and marker pens.

### HOW TO USE IT

1 Agree on the issue(s) to be discussed – these should be subtopics of a bigger idea.
2 Divide the group into smaller groups, maximum seven per group, plus a recorder (who is also the small group facilitator).
3 Assign an issue to each group.
4 Each group brainstorms its issue.
5 The recorder facilitates and records all ideas.
6 At a given time/signal, the recorder moves to the next group.
7 The recorder reviews the issues/responses of the new group.
8 The groups begin brainstorming again around a new idea, building on the thinking from the last idea.
9 Repeat steps 5 to 8 until each group has discussed all the issues.
10 Allow the recorders/groups time to draw all the ideas together into key themes or strands.
11 In plenary, ask recorders to present the key ideas coming from their groups. You may need to rank the ideas.

## POINTS TO WATCH OUT FOR

Much of the success of this and other large-scale techniques is due to the planning. Plan well ahead of the event, send very clear instructions about the purpose, timing, requirements, expectations and benefits of the session.

## TOOL 54 STARBURSTING

### WHAT THE TOOL IS

Like *Tough questions* **(see Tool 2)**, *Starbursting* is a team activity that ensures that all the right questions are asked before any solutions are explored. Often, an apparently silly question opens up a whole new series of questions. When *Starbursting* works well, the person posing the question realises that they have much more work to do before attempting to find a solution or that the problem is more complex than they had imagined.

### WHEN TO USE IT

■ Before attempting to find a solution to a complex issue with many sub-strands.

### WHAT YOU WILL NEED

■ Flipchart paper and marker pens or paper and pens (depending upon the number of participants).

### HOW TO USE IT

You can use this technique on your own, but it is more fun and more productive with one or more small groups of, say, four people per group.

1   Create a six-pointed star on a piece of paper – you may choose to use ordinary office paper or, for larger groups, flipchart paper. Label the points of the star with question words: Who? What? Where? Why? When? How?

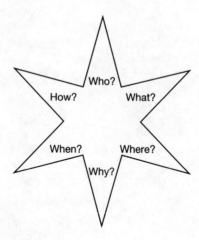

2   Brainstorm questions about the topic, starting with each of the question words around the star. Generate as many relevant questions as you can.

3   Do not attempt to answer the questions. At this stage, you are only generating questions.

4   Write the questions so that they radiate from the points of the star.

5   If several groups are taking part, ask one group to read all its questions, prompted by a particular question word, and then ask other groups to add any questions not posed by the first group. Now move to another group and let them lead with their questions, prompted by another question word, with other groups adding to it. Repeat for each question word.

6   Collect the *Starbursting* diagrams and, after the session, collate the questions and distribute them to participants.

## VARIANTS

■   You can either generate one set of questions or use each set of questions to stimulate the creation of a new set.

■   Break a large group into smaller groups. Either let each group explore the same issue or give different issues (or different aspects of the same issue) to each smaller group and ask them to share their questions in plenary.

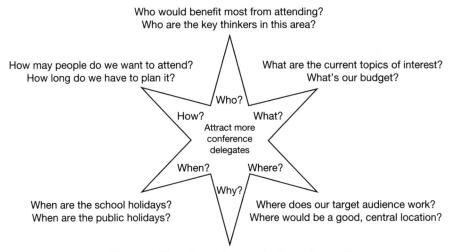

## POINTS TO WATCH OUT FOR

In any group there are know-alls who will try to dismiss some questions as too obvious. Make it clear at the outset that, no matter how obvious the answer to a question, it should be added to the sheet. The aim is to create the most comprehensive list possible of relevant questions and it is important to capture them all because questions spawn new questions.

Encourage participants to add questions to their sheets as quickly as they think of them. Rather than try to exhaust all 'Who?' questions before moving to 'What?' questions, they should call out any question that occurs to them, as it occurs to them so that nothing is lost. They can revisit each question word as often as they like.

TOOL 55    # OPEN SPACE

## WHAT THE TOOL IS

*Open space* is a large-scale, collaborative problem-solving methodology in which the group participating effectively creates its own agenda. Individuals post their problems on a notice board and then convene breakout meetings in which the problems are discussed and the owner takes notes of ideas. Participants can wander freely between breakout groups, offering help and moving on when they feel they have nothing more to contribute.

## WHEN TO USE IT

- For strategic planning.
- For organisational design.
- For any decision making that will affect people cross-functionally.

## WHAT YOU WILL NEED

- A circle of chairs for participants.
- Signs indicating the meeting locations.
- Breakout spaces or rooms for smaller meetings.
- A blank wall for the agenda.
- A news wall.
- Paper on which to write session topics or questions.
- Pens, pencils, markers.

## HOW TO USE IT

1  Bring the group together in a circle.
2  Distribute paper to each participant.
3  Welcome the participants and explain the process.
4  Invite anyone with a concern or an issue to be resolved to write it on a piece of paper, come into the centre of the circle and announce the concern to the group.
5  Those who express concerns are described as 'conveners' and, having announced their concerns, each places their paper on an 'agenda' wall with a place to meet and a time slot. Ideally, this should be prepared in advance of the session, with small placards on the wall listing each breakout room/area, so that the conveners can place their written concerns under a location name and add their start time.
6  Participants note the times and locations of the sessions that interest them.
7  The conveners start their sessions and interested parties come and join them.

**8** Each group appoints a recorder to capture the important points and post their reports on a 'news wall'. Reports will be collated and fed back in a plenary session.

**9** After a break, groups might move to a convergence stage in which they attach actions plans to the points raised.

**10** The group comes back together in a circle in which participants are invited to share comments, insights and agreed actions arising from the process.

If you find yourself in a breakout meeting to which you can contribute nothing or in which you are learning nothing, then exercise the *Law of Two Feet* and move to another session to which you believe you can contribute something.

THE PRINCIPLES OF OPEN SPACE

The originators of *Open space* believe that:

- Whoever comes are the right people.
- Whenever it starts is the right time.
- Whatever happens is the only thing that could have happened.
- When it is over, it is over.

There are some flaws in these basic principles. In reality, there may be too little time for the right people to take part in each small group discussion and the timing may not be appropriate for everyone. The other two ideas suggest some kind of inevitability about the process and outcomes that somewhat fly in the face of common sense.

POINTS TO WATCH OUT FOR

There is a great deal of literature both in book form and on the internet about the art of hosting.

Note that the originators of *Open space*, and a number of other methods for facilitating large group discussions, use a language that may alienate hard-headed business people. For example, gathering information is described as 'harvesting', a facilitator is described as a 'host' and a participant's choice to move between discussion groups is described as *the Law of Two Feet*. For some, this language is a step too far. If you can move beyond the language, however, open space and related methods include some great techniques and principles for large-scale meeting facilitation.

Just because the originators of these processes use what may appear to some as New Age language, does not mean that you have to adopt it. Gauge your participants carefully and use language appropriate to them.

Any major event (and use of this technique *is* a major event) requires a great deal of planning and strong, focused facilitation. If you have never run an event like this before, consider bringing in an experienced external facilitator the first time, work with the facilitator and build your confidence to lead future events.

REFERENCE

Owen, H. (2008) *Open Space Technology: A User's Guide.* San Francisco: Berrett-Koehler Publishers.

## TOOL 56  WORLD CAFÉ

### WHAT THE TOOL IS

World Café was designed as a process to facilitate large meetings, give people an equal voice and invite contributions from everyone.

Small groups sitting at café-style tables discuss a problem for a set time period. One person 'hosts' each table group. At a given signal, participants move to other tables where the host talks through the discussions of the last group. Either the same question is repeated or a related question is discussed. Repeat the process, collect the ideas, present them in plenary and rank the solutions the groups have produced.

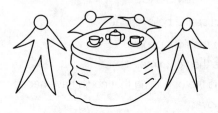

### WHEN TO USE IT

- For strategic planning.
- For organisational design.
- For any decision making that will affect people cross-functionally.

### WHAT YOU WILL NEED

- A large workspace, set up in café or cabaret style.
- Flipchart paper and pens. (It can be useful to place a piece of flipchart paper and marker pens on each table and encourage people to sketch their ideas as they discuss them.)
- Paper and pens on each table.

### HOW TO USE IT

1  *Setting:* Setup is usually café style, with small tables for four or five people. Provide paper, pens and, possibly, a 'talking object' (only the person who is holding it may speak). Each table has a host, who usually stays at the same table throughout the process.
2  *Welcome and introduction:* The event host welcomes everyone, sets the scene for the discussion and describes the process.
3  *Question:* A question is posed, related to the main topic of the discussion.

**4** *Small group rounds:* Three or more 20-minute rounds of conversation based around the question. At the end of 20 minutes, the table members move to other tables (spreading out across tables rather than moving as a group). As the new group arrives, the table host talks through the thoughts of the last group.

**5** *Question:* Either the same question is repeated or a new question is posed, which develops the theme already discussed.

**6** *Harvest:* Insights and results are collated and presented in plenary through a variety of methods, which may include graphical recording, clustering of ideas on a board and ranking of solutions.

## THE OPERATING PRINCIPLES OF WORLD CAFÉ

- Create a hospitable space.
- Explore questions that matter (to the participants, their organisation or beyond).
- Encourage each person's contributions.
- Connect diverse people and ideas.
- Listen together for patterns, insights and deeper questions.
- Make collective knowledge visible.

In this and other collective contribution processes, it is said that we should 'listen with attention and speak with intention'. This means that participants listen carefully to what others are saying and speak in response to what they have heard, rather than waiting for a space to say what they want to say.

## POINTS TO WATCH OUT FOR

As for *Open space* **(see Tool 55)**, any major event (and use of this technique *is* a major event) requires a great deal of planning and strong, focused facilitation. If you have never run an event like this before, consider bringing in an experienced external facilitator the first time, work with the facilitator and build your confidence to lead future events.

## REFERENCE

Brown, J. and Isaacs, D. (2005) *The World Café: Shaping Our Futures Through Conversations That Matter.* San Francisco: Berrett-Koehler Publishers.

## TOOL 57  PRO-ACTION CAFÉ

### WHAT THE TOOL IS

This is a powerful technique used for collaborative problem solving with a large group and is built on *World café* **(see Tool 56)** and *Open space* **(see Tool 55)** principles. Individuals raise issues that they would like to discuss, based on a central theme. The technique allows exploration of the quest behind the question and what everyone needs to know to make the picture more complete.

### WHEN TO USE IT

- When you need to move relatively quickly from problem solving to action.
- For strategic planning.
- For organisational design.
- For any decision making that will affect people cross-functionally.

### WHAT YOU WILL NEED

- A large circle of chairs, one per participant, and additional tables to accommodate small groups of three or four people. If this is not possible, participants can move the chairs from the circle to marked areas of the room to create smaller groups.
- Flipchart paper and marker pens.
- An agenda matrix on a flipchart on which conveners can write their questions.

| Table | Name | Questions, issues, projects |
|---|---|---|
| 1 | | |
| 2 | | |
| 3 | | |
| 4 | | |
| 5 | | |
| 6 | | |
| 7 | | |
| 8 | | |
| 9 | | |

### HOW TO USE IT

1  Everyone meets in a circle to understand the purpose of the session.

2  Participants consider in silence if there is a question they would like to explore.

3  They are asked to share it and invite others to work with them on it. Those who do not raise questions are asked to work with those who do.

4   Each person with an issue to explore stands up, states their issue and writes it on an agenda, then chooses the number of the table at which they will meet. Ideally, each table should have a host and three or four other people.

5   Three rounds of conversation for 20 to 30 minutes each, each focusing on a specific question to broaden and deepen the process before converging. A five-minute break between rounds.

    **Round 1:** *What is the quest behind the question?* Dig under the surface of what we already know to understand the initial question better.

    **Round 2:** *What is missing?* What do we need to know to make the picture more complete?

    **Round 3:** *Next steps and key learnings.* In the final round, the convener remains at the table and the groups rotate to the next table to hear the thoughts so far and offer fine-tuning and help. The hosts and participants assimilate what they have learnt and take away actions.

6   Feedback in a circle. Everyone gathers in a seated circle in which the hosts describe what happened at their tables and what they will take away from the discussions. If time permits, others may wish to share their experience of the activity. To control the flow of conversation in the feedback session, some groups use a 'talking object' – the object can be anything at all, and only the person holding it may speak. For some, this may be taking things a little too far: it has the advantage of ensuring that people do not interrupt each other, but can make discussion a little stilted and over-formalised.

## POINTS TO WATCH OUT FOR

As for the last two methods, any major event (and use of this technique *is* a major event) requires a great deal of planning and strong, focused facilitation. If you have never run an event like this before, consider bringing in an experienced external facilitator the first time, work with the facilitator and build your confidence to lead future events.

# PART 5

# PROBLEM-SOLVING BUSINESS GAMES

# WHEN AND HOW TO USE BUSINESS GAMES

Some people believe that 'games' have no place in serious organisations. Meetings are serious events with a serious purpose. I could not disagree more strongly! Children learn through play and so do adults. Our problem is that we do not necessarily allow adults to learn the same way as children. Children learn by play, by activity and by making mistakes. Rather than give up at the first sign of failure, they persevere. How many of us would pursue the art of walking if it were something we learnt to do only as adults? At the first fall, most of us would think, 'Well, I'm not trying that again!'

The art of using business games is to ensure that a game has a serious purpose, and that the purpose either becomes apparent during play, or is brought to the surface in the debrief that follows the game.

The trick of introducing games into 'serious' organisations is not to call them games, but 'activities' and do them anyway. I have been designing and using games in training and meetings for years and, only very occasionally, have I encountered people unwilling to join in.

If you can use a game to stimulate thinking and create solutions to problems, then it is as viable as any other problem-solving technique. (Just do not mention the word 'game'!)

## TOOL 58 RETIREMENT SPEECHES

### WHAT THE TOOL IS
This is a role-playing game that frees participants from the constraints of the present to imagine a better future.

### WHEN TO USE IT
- When a group is struggling to see how it can improve its working methods, this role-playing game can be enormously helpful.

### WHAT YOU WILL NEED
- A large workspace.
- Paper and pens (for small groups to plan their role play).

### HOW TO USE IT
Ask small groups to project themselves into the future, imagining that it is their retirement day and they have, throughout their working lives, created a great place to work, a highly dynamic team, a place with seamless and efficient tools and processes (or whatever is pertinent to the group).

They now have to imagine that they are going to make a presentation to a group of new joiners to the team/department, explaining what they did to make it so good. They actually present to the larger group.

In presenting the ideal future, effectively by looking backwards, they free themselves from the constraints they would see if simply asked to look forward. Small groups prepare, present to others in plenary and, after each small group has presented, ideas are ranked, voted on and explored in more depth to turn them from abstract concepts into practical reality.

### POINTS TO WATCH OUT FOR
Sometimes a group becomes so caught up in the creative freedom that this method brings that they lose sight of reality, inventing a future that is beyond reach. This has both positive and negative spin-offs. If their invented future is too outlandish, then the

gap between the present and future will seem unbridgeable. However, in imagining a future without known constraints, they start to believe that real change is possible and from the often bizarre ideas suggested comes an imaginably better future.

Try using the PMI technique **(see Tool 4)** to explore in more detail some of the seeds of possibility sown here.

# CONVINCE ME

## WHAT THE TOOL IS

This is a debating technique in which participants show their agreement or opposition by moving physically towards or away from each other. Because participants are told which viewpoint to adopt, they cannot simply argue vehemently in favour of their own ideas. This forces them immediately to see a question from a different perspective, which may free up their thinking, if not to agree with the other side then at least to understand it and make some concessions to it.

## WHEN TO USE IT

■ When there are opposing forces in an organisation and simple discussion or debate has not yielded a solution.

## WHAT YOU WILL NEED

■ A large workspace/meeting room, with tables removed.

## HOW TO USE IT

1   Two teams are asked to adopt opposing ideas of how to solve a problem. Whether or not the stance they take reflects their own thinking does not matter for these purposes. Their job is to produce a well-reasoned argument from the perspective allocated to their team.
2   They stand in lines facing each other, at opposite sides of a room.
3   Anyone can present an argument to persuade the other team to come over to their point of view.
4   As individuals hear a compelling argument, they take a step towards the other team.

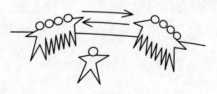

5   When the majority of members of one team have stepped over the halfway point between the two teams, the first round is over.
6   Now small, mixed groups work together to discuss how the winning solution may be implemented.

## POINTS TO WATCH OUT FOR

Participants must agree to play their part from the standpoint allocated to them, regardless of whether they would naturally concur with it. Sometimes they present only half-hearted arguments because they consider that they have been placed in the wrong team.

If you suspect that any participants will be opposed to being told which team to join, then you may have to group them according to common belief. The upside is that you will have a good debate. The downside is that it does not push people quite so strongly towards understanding another group's perspective.

TOOL 60 **EVOLUTION**

## WHAT THE TOOL IS

The evolutionary theory is based on the survival of the fittest. This tool is designed for deep exploration of the strongest and weakest areas of an organisation to gauge what should be developed and what should not be allowed to survive

## WHEN TO USE IT

This is a tool for senior decision makers working in conjunction with functional leaders at a time when there is concern about the direction an organisation is taking; for example, when there has been:

- a downturn in profits;
- a decrease in take-up of services;
- a fall in the level of charitable contributions received;
- some reputational damage to the organisation;
- anything that signals that the organisation is not working as well as it should.

## WHAT YOU WILL NEED

- A flipchart and marker pens per team.

## HOW TO USE IT

Teams work to establish the aspects of their business that are strongest and so most likely to survive:

- What can they do to ensure that survival?
- How can they develop the strongest areas to be stronger?
- Is there a danger in focusing too much on a limited range of areas of the organisation and so missing something important elsewhere?
- What happens to the weaker areas?
- Can they be strengthened or should they be removed?
- What would be the effect (in cost, time, materials, etc.) of shoring up the weaker areas?

- What would be the ramifications of closing down the weaker areas?
- What would 'business as usual' look like if the stronger areas were developed and the weaker areas abandoned, scaled down or terminated?

## POINTS TO WATCH OUT FOR

It must be handled extremely sensitively because some participants may feel their work areas (and possibly their livelihood) are threatened. It works best with a group of senior people who are able to set territorial gains and personal agendas to one side and work for the benefit of the organisation.

## TOOL 61  IT'S IN THE NEWS

### WHAT THE TOOL IS

By imagining themselves as teams of investigative journalists, small teams focus on fact finding to gather as much information as possible to resolve complex business problems.

### WHEN TO USE IT

- To resolve complex problems involving many stakeholders.

### WHAT YOU WILL NEED

- Paper and pens.
- Time (the method is conducted in two parts, with a time gap between them).

### HOW TO USE IT

1  A large group of people from a mixed range of grades is broken into smaller groups.
2  Each small group imagines itself to be a team of investigative journalists.

3  Small groups write their business problem as though it were a newspaper headline and then write a brief article about it based entirely on current knowledge, without surmise or assumption.
4  As they do so, they should note separately just how much they really know, what they need to know, who they should talk to, etc. and then map this back to the real problem, setting out their plan to investigate further, talk in more depth to stakeholders and interested parties to get a more complete picture in order to solve the problem.
5  They should agree a time period in which they will conduct their investigation, write the complete article and get back to each other to present their articles and discuss their findings with the larger group.

### POINTS TO WATCH OUT FOR

There is a danger that between the first and second meeting, teams write sensationalist articles because they get too carried away with the idea of being journalists and lose sight of the objective, which is fact finding to aid problem solving or decision making.

## TOOL 62  THE TRIAL

### WHAT THE TOOL IS

This is a courtroom-style activity in which participants present arguments for and against the solution to a problem, call witnesses and, finally, the group assesses the evidence and votes in favour of or against the solution.

### WHEN TO USE IT

■ When you need a variety of views on a critical or complex organisational issue. The preparation for this technique can be time-consuming and it is a non-trivial method of examining an important issue in depth before reaching one or more decisions on how to proceed.

### WHAT YOU WILL NEED

■ A disinterested person to act as judge.

### HOW TO USE IT

1  All interested parties are brought together to discuss an organisational problem.
2  Brainstorm solutions to the problem and use a ranking method to assess the favourite solution.
3  Appoint a recorder and judge.
4  Divide the remaining group into two smaller teams – one for the prosecution and one for the defence.
5  Each team must appoint a leader who will, ultimately, represent it in the trial.
6  The prosecution team must amass as much evidence as it can to find flaws in the solution, and appoint key witnesses from within the team to speak on their behalf.
7  The defending team must amass as much evidence as it can to support the solution, and appoint key witnesses from within the group to speak on its behalf.
8  The *trial* is convened.
9  The judge asks the lead prosecutor to present the team's case against the solution (the aim being to expose its flaws). The prosecutor may call witnesses to support the team's case.

**10** At the judge's behest, the recorder will note key arguments in favour of the solution on a flipchart headed *'For',* visible to all participants.

**11** The lead defender presents the case in support of the solution (the aim being to highlight its benefits). The defender may call witnesses to support the team's case.

**12** At the judge's behest, the recorder will note key arguments against the solution on a flipchart headed *'Against',* visible to all participants.

**13** When each side has presented its case, the lead prosecutor and lead defender may summarise their arguments.

**14** At this point, the official trial is over and the evidence is assessed using the force field analysis method **(see Tool 1).**

POINTS TO WATCH OUT FOR

Ensure that whoever acts as *judge* has no vested interest in the outcome of the trial. It may be worth recruiting the judge from an organisational group not directly affected by the issue being 'tried'.

## TOOL 63    TORTOISE AND HARE

### WHAT THE TOOL IS

In a world of sound bites and quick wins, sometimes it is useful to step back and consider the effects of a slower approach to resolving a problem. In *Tortoise and hare,* more immediate, rapid solutions are contrasted with slower, longer-term approaches. The aim is to develop a range of solutions that work in the short, medium and longer term to give depth to a solution.

### WHEN TO USE IT

- For planning – whether strategic or operational.
- For organisational design.

### WHAT YOU WILL NEED

- Two flipcharts and marker pens.

### HOW TO USE IT

1   Divide a group into two teams. One team is the hares, the other the tortoises. Each team works independently of the other to discuss solutions to the same business problem.

2 Hares must find quick wins, easy solutions and rapid approaches to solving the problem. Tortoises must find medium- and longer-term solutions to the same problem.

3 Each presents to the other in plenary and, after a facilitated discussion on the merits and demerits of each suggestion, ideas are ranked/voted on and, where possible, combined.

## POINTS TO WATCH OUT FOR

You need a strong facilitator to ensure that the more dominant participants do not overshadow quieter ones with good ideas.

## TOOL 64 ART GALLERY

### WHAT THE TOOL IS

In highly logical, process-driven organisations, problems tend to be solved through tried and tested analytical approaches. *Art gallery* helps participants break away from a left-brained, logical approach and become more creative in their thinking.

### WHEN TO USE IT

- When standard approaches to a problem are not yielding any new insights.
- With creative groups who have rare opportunities to demonstrate that creativity.
- With non-creative groups who need a way of breaking away from logical, structured thinking.

### WHAT YOU WILL NEED

- Paper and pens for each participant.
- Wall space for displaying artwork.
- Reusable adhesive or tape.

### HOW TO USE IT

1. State the problem to be resolved.
2. Participants sketch whatever comes into their heads as they think about the problem. They can focus on any aspect of the problem and illustrate it however they wish.
3. Display their artworks in a 'gallery' and, as participants view each other's pictures, they use them to stimulate their thinking about solutions to the problem.
4. Facilitate a discussion to allow participants to air the ideas and solutions that have come out of their tour of the 'gallery'.

### VARIANTS

Whilst participants are discussing a problem and possible solutions, ask someone with artistic ability to sit back from the main discussion and sketch anything that occurs to him/her, then display the artist's pictures. Participants study the pictures and see and discuss the new ideas they stimulate.

### POINTS TO WATCH OUT FOR

Typically, at the outset, many of the participants will claim that they cannot draw. Make it clear that they are not going to be judged on the quality of their artistic endeavours and that the idea is simply to use the creative side of their brain to generate fresh insights into a problem.

## TOOL 65   PROVERBIAL PROBLEM SOLVING

### WHAT THE TOOL IS
Small groups are given a number of proverbs and must use them to stimulate thinking about issues within their team or organisation.

### WHEN TO USE IT

■ When a team is struggling to find insight into organisational issues using more conventional methods.

### WHAT YOU WILL NEED

■ A printed list of proverbs – one copy per participant. You can find comprehensive lists on many websites. Select around 10 that are relatively easy to understand.

### HOW TO USE IT

1 Compile and print a list of proverbs. You might like to include, for example:
   ■ 'Too many cooks spoil the broth.'
   ■ 'A little bit of knowledge is a dangerous thing.'
   ■ 'Better safe than sorry.'
   ■ 'A rolling stone gathers no moss.'
2 Distribute the list to participants, who may work alone, in pairs or threes.
3 Present the problem to them and ask them to use the proverbs to stimulate thinking about it, whether to create solutions or simply to ensure that they are asking the right questions.

For example:
   ■ 'Too many cooks spoil the broth.' Where do we have too many people involved in a process that requires fewer people's involvement?
   ■ 'A little bit of knowledge is a dangerous thing.' Where do our people lack information, knowledge or skills necessary to do their jobs better?
   ■ 'Better safe than sorry.' Are we managing risk appropriately? Are our health and safety measures appropriate? Are we being too risk-averse/over cautious in some areas?
   ■ 'A rolling stone gathers no moss.' Are there ways in which we can act quickly and effectively, with low risk, to get ahead of our competitors?

### POINTS TO WATCH OUT FOR
Ensure that participants actually understand the proverbs!

TOOL 66 # THERE ARE NO RULES

## WHAT THE TOOL IS

This is a structured way of revisiting long-standing rules and procedures to gain fresh insight and dispense with the idea that we retain processes simply because 'we've always done it that way'.

## WHEN TO USE IT

- When bureaucracy seems to be overshadowing common sense.
- When 'the way we do things here' has not been re-evaluated for a long time.
- When the organisation is in danger of becoming a tick-box culture, driven by process instead of using minimal processes to avoid chaos and using the processes as a stepping stone to higher performance.

## WHAT YOU WILL NEED

- Paper and pens.

## HOW TO USE IT

1 Small groups are each allocated a process, procedure or a set of house rules.
2 They must decide on its original purpose, then effectively tear it up and start again with a simplified set of rules or governing principles that address the original purpose or problem.
3 Each group presents in plenary and the larger group determines whether:
    - the new rules/principles are an effective replacement for the original;
    - some of the ideas the activity generates can be incorporated into the original rules to simplify or refine them;
    - in fact, no rules would be the best option, leaving an issue to the integrity of those involved rather than dictating how it should be done.

## POINTS TO WATCH OUT FOR

Ensure that the participants understand the business context for the processes that they are refining. If they have scant knowledge about the underlying business need, they may innocently remove a step that is vital in the process.

Ideally, ensure that you have some subject experts in the larger group who are open to reform of systems and processes and not likely to defend them out of familiarity or a sense of 'we've always done it that way'.

TOOL 67 **DOCUMENTARY**

## WHAT THE TOOL IS

Teams must create a radio- or TV-style 'documentary' about a business problem, to include a statement of the issue, interviews and possible solutions.

## WHEN TO USE IT

■ To explore a business problem creatively and in depth.

## WHAT YOU WILL NEED

■ A workspace sufficiently large to allow several teams to work independently of each other or breakout rooms (one per team) and a plenary room.

## HOW TO USE IT

1  Split a larger group into smaller teams.
2  Allocate a business problem to each team (either distinctly different problems or subsets of the same problem).
3  Give teams a time limit in which they have to create a radio- or TV-style 'documentary' that explores the issue and possible solutions to it

4  Each team enacts its documentary in front of the larger group combining presentation and interviews.
5  You may then choose to use other methods to assess or further explore the solutions presented and, if appropriate, vote on the best one or best combination of solutions.

## POINTS TO WATCH OUT FOR

■ Participants often start with some cynicism about this activity or fear of appearing stupid (a common fear in any role play). In setting the scene, explain that this is not about acting or playing a part but simply a medium for exploring an idea in more depth.
■ Beware, too, of the show-offs who dominate the small groups, want centre stage and rather miss the business point of the activity.

TOOL 68    # PITCH PERFECT

## WHAT THE TOOL IS

This is a competitive process in which participants, working in teams, are given a problem to solve and then pitch their solutions to an expert panel that determines the best solution. It is based on a British television programme (*Dragons' Den*) in which entrepreneurs pitch to a panel of wealthy investors to get funding to develop or market their products.

## WHEN TO USE IT

- When a number of smaller groups has worked on the same problem and believe their solution is the best.

## WHAT YOU WILL NEED

- Paper and pens.
- A small prize for the winning team (optional).

## HOW TO USE IT

1    Appoint a panel of experienced people and allocate large amounts of notional money to each one of them – say, 100,000 of your local currency.
2    Small groups each prepare a solution to a different, pressing business problem, then one or two from each group pitch their solution to the panel of experts.
3    Give each group a time limit (of, say, five minutes) for their pitch.
4    Experts question the presenters about their solutions and can then allocate their notional money to ideas based on their merit, or choose to opt out if they believe a solution has no real merit (is not worth pursuing). An expert refusing to invest explains the reasons not to invest and declares, 'I'm out!'
5    The solutions with the highest 'investment' of points are then taken back to the wider group and other techniques used to explore how they can be implemented in practice.

## VARIANTS

Each group works on the same business problem and presents its suggested solution to the experts. Experts allocate notional money (points) to each solution. The one with the highest investment is then developed in practice.

Offer a small prize to the 'winning' team.

## POINTS TO WATCH OUT FOR

Emphasise from the outset that the aim is to produce something viable, not to impress.

PART 6

# SHARING AND IMPLEMENTING SOLUTIONS

# SHARING SOLUTIONS

I t is all very well involving groups of people in creative processes to generate ideas, solutions to problems and new ways of working. But what happens when you have those ideas? How do you determine which are worth pursuing?

In this section, you will find:

- a wealth of methods of collecting (sometimes described as 'harvesting') ideas generated in a collaborative problem-solving session;
- ways of ranking those ideas and voting on them so that the best of them can be implemented.

## SHARING AND 'HARVESTING' TECHNIQUES

You have spent time solving a problem in small groups and are now asking those groups to report back in plenary. Here are some ways of gathering information from them:

- One group presents its thoughts; others add anything not covered by the first group. This is a quick way of getting feedback. Be careful – if one group declares all its ideas, others may feel that they wasted their time in the process because their ideas were not heard

- Each group presents one key/significant point ('cream off the top'). This is useful for making people feel that they are equally important in the process. One point to watch – if one group presents a point that another group had prepared to present, that group will then enter into private (and distracting) conversation as they debate their second best point and will not hear the other groups' contributions.

- Groups document their ideas on a flipchart; one person from each group stays with the flipchart; groups rotate around flipcharts and the person who remained with the flipchart presents to each group in turn. Do this at speed. If each group effectively duplicates the same points, the tour can be rather dull. It works best when each group has worked on a sub-topic of the main theme.

- Ideas are ranged around the wall like art exhibits; groups or individuals take time to walk round and examine the 'exhibits' before discussion of the best ideas.

- Teams present three things they have learned/decided/concluded. Again, if they have all concluded the same things, the repetition may be boring, but if you ask each to declare something different from the others, teams may have to debate what they are going to say whilst others are presenting their ideas.

- One person from each team has 60 seconds to summarise their ideas. A variant on this comes from a long-standing BBC radio game show called *Just a Minute* in which contestants must speak about a given subject for 60 seconds without hesitation, deviation or repetition. Other contestants may challenge any of these transgressions! It puts people on the spot, but it adds a fun element and ensures focus.

- Teams present their three/five top tips. Again, this may lead to repetition or side discussions.
- Teams present how to do something entirely wrong, so that the rest of the group can learn how to do it right.
- 'The most important thing is . . .' and 'The least important thing is . . .'
- Groups present opposite viewpoints as a precursor to discussion. This is useful in ensuring a well-rounded, informed debate.
- 'Taboo' – describe a subject without mentioning certain key words (determined in advance by the facilitator). The rest of group must guess the words being described.
- Create an aide memoir or mnemonic to help others to remember key points.

You may choose to photograph flipcharts and distribute the photos after the event, so that everyone feels that they made a valid contribution and ideas of merit that did not make the 'cut' are not lost.

## TABLE GROUP COMPETITIONS

Set competitions between table groups/pairs/threes and ask delegates to vote for any group other than their own. Here are some examples:

- The table group with the greatest number of answers to a question.
- The table group with the cleverest answer to a question.
- The table group with the most thoughtful solution to a problem.
- The table group with the most creative solution to a problem.
- The table group with the most practical solution to a problem.
- The first table group to achieve something.

## GRAPHICAL 'HARVESTING'

In some circles, capturing ideas from a group is described as 'harvesting'. Drawings, diagrams and cartoons can be a wonderful way to capture ideas and often stimulate further thinking: our left brains handle the rational side of our discussions and pictures tap into the creative, right side of the brain to help us to make more connections.

You do not have to be a great artist to capture ideas. Take a look at these videos for ideas:

http://bit.ly/1Ak6lVL

http://bit.ly/1bdspN9

To develop a library of graphical ideas, see this video:
https://www.youtube.com/watch?v=S5DJC6LaOCl

## TIPS

- Put flipchart sheets on tables or use paper tablecloths during problem-solving meetings. Encourage people to scribble and sketch as they discuss an issue. Often, new ideas are stimulated by the pictures.

- Put two or three flipchart stands in a row, so participants can capture big ideas across several charts in parallel.

- Ask if participants can think of a metaphor for the subject they are discussing and use it as a visual representation or backdrop for the harvested ideas.

- Ask one or two participants with reasonable artistic flair to capture ideas during a conversation or discussion.

- Treat the visual harvest as a giant doodle, focusing more on capturing ideas than on the beauty of the artwork, and you will find it starts to flow.

- Look online for symbols and have those to hand when you create the graphical harvest.

- Make your pictures colourful so they are attractive to participants.

## RANKING AND VOTING

You have worked with others to find multiple solutions to a problem, and now you need to decide upon the best one(s) to implement. Here are some methods of voting on and ranking those ideas:

- *Show of hands:* The simplest voting method is a show of hands. Let us say four small groups have each presented a solution: ask the groups to vote on each idea in turn by a show of hands. They may only vote once and, importantly, not for their own group's idea.

- *Yes or No:* The second easiest method is to ask all in favour to call 'Yes' and then all against to call 'No'. The obvious danger is that, if the vote is close, it may be difficult to detect which vote had more supporters.

- *Sticky dots:* Give participants sticky coloured paper dots. They are allowed to allocate a fixed number of dots (say three or five) to collected ideas. They may distribute them in any way they wish – for example, giving all five dots to a single idea, one each to five ideas or three dots to one and two to another, etc. This is a great way to rank ideas or solutions. It engages people physically in the act of allocating the dots, it allows them to vote for ideas with relative anonymity and ensures that the dominant participants have no more power in the voting than anyone else involved.

- *Red card/green card:* Give each participant a red card and a green card. Voting is done by holding up the appropriate card – red for 'no', green for 'yes'.

- *Anonymous voting:* For sensitive issues, you may consider anonymous voting. Each solution is given a letter or number. Each participant writes the letter or number corresponding to their preferred option on a slip of paper and posts it in a box.

- *Rank by letter:* A variant on the anonymous vote is to ascribe a letter to each proposed solution and ask the participants to write the letters in descending order of preference and hand them in to be collated.

- *Stand up/sit down:* You may ask participants to stand up to show support of a particular solution or ask all to stand up and those in favour to remain standing, whilst those against sit down.

# IMPLEMENTING SOLUTIONS

You have framed a problem beautifully, gathered together a team of interested parties to help you resolve it, chosen and executed the ideal problem-solving method and your solution creates a need for change – change to a system, a process, a method of doing something, a way of thinking, the structure of a team or even an organisation. Having the ideal solution is not enough – now you have to sell the idea to others.

Whilst this book is about problem solving rather than change management, the act of implementing a solution can be a major problem in its own right, so let us explore some ways of implementing solutions and making them work.

Let us start by dismissing a major myth about change management. This is the *change curve,* espoused by change managers and management consultants many years ago to describe the stages that people go through when they encounter change at work. The curve was described originally by Elisabeth Kübler-Ross[1], an expert in 'near-death studies', who worked extensively with people told that they had a terminal illness. She talked about the five emotional stages (denial, anger, bargaining, depression, acceptance) that those who knew they had little time to live might go through. Significantly, she said that not everyone would go through all the stages, nor necessarily in a prescribed order. Management consultants seized upon this and determined that, if dying people go through these stages (after all, dying is a big change . . .), then people facing change at work must go through the same stages. In my many years working with two of the world's biggest consultancies and training people who faced change, I rarely saw anyone conform to this curve, unless their livelihood was threatened. The truth is, if an organisation has good managers and leaders, rarely should any change be a surprise: good managers and leaders communicate constantly with their staff who, as a result, know what is happening in their organisation.

In reality, there probably *are* five reactions to change, which we outlined briefly earlier in reference to preparing the ground for problem solving – but they are not those outlined by Kübler-Ross! Now let us look at them in more detail:

| Active acceptance | | Passive acceptance |
|---|---|---|
| | Indifference | |
| Active resistance | | Passive resistance |

**Indifference:** A remarkably high number of people are indifferent to change. They have seen it all before! Change is not new, not remarkable and often not terribly interesting. The most emotional statements you are likely to hear from them are 'Whatever!' or 'Here we go again'.

---

[1] *On Death and Dying* (1969)

**Active acceptance:** There are many reasons why someone might actively (and vocally) accept a change, some perhaps surprising. These include:

- They see that it is a good idea.
- They do not know any better.
- They see benefits for themselves in the new regime.
- They trust their manager who has got things right before and has probably got it right this time.
- They are sycophants who will agree with their manager for purely self-serving reasons.
- They are swayed by one of their trusted colleagues who agrees with the change.
- Most of their friends believe the change is ok, and they are swayed by peer pressure.

In a sense, it does not matter what motivates the active acceptor to agree with the change – they make all the right noises and are prepared to vocalise their support for the new idea.

**Active resistance:** There are many reasons why someone might actively (and vocally) resist a change. These include:

- They see that it is a bad idea.
- They know that it will not work. They have a long corporate memory and have seen similar schemes fail in the past. They are not negative in their outlook, but realistic in their appraisal of your solution. Enlist them as change agents – they will help you to make it work.
- They see no benefits for themselves in the new regime.
- They do not trust their manager because of past failures, predicting that this will work no better than the last hare-brained scheme.
- They are swayed by one of their trusted colleagues who disagrees with the change.
- Most of their friends believe the change is flawed and they are swayed by peer pressure.

You need to understand at an individual level why these people resist the change and are prepared to vocalise their resistance, then deal with them individually.

**Passive acceptance:** Passive acceptors accept the change and simply get on and implement it. They do not talk about it but you will find them quietly doing what you have asked them to do. It can be useful to get them to vocalise their support of the change to sway some of the indifferent ones towards some level of acceptance.

**Passive resistance:** Passive resistors are the most dangerous people in times of change. Publicly, they may appear to agree to the change but, privately, will either do nothing to implement it or subtly sabotage it. You need to discover what drives this behaviour in them individually and manage them one at a time through the change process.

Once you are aware of individuals' reactions to change, you can plan your approach to talking to them. The key here is to understand individual reactions rather than expecting that a whole team will react the same way.

REASONS WHY CHANGE FAILS

There is a vast number of reasons why change may fail. Here is just a small sample:

■ The change was silly/wrong.

■ The change was designed to fulfil a senior person's personal agenda.

■ It was poorly communicated.

■ The context was not properly explained.

■ Change fatigue – too many changes in too short a time period.

■ It reverses something else that recently changed.

■ The ripple effects were not understood and the change has unforeseen consequences elsewhere.

■ It was badly implemented.

■ Leaders fail to 'walk the talk', paying lip service to the change, but not demonstrating that they, too, are changing their own working practices.

■ The change is at odds with the culture.

■ The organisational structure cannot support the change.

■ There is an absence of systems and processes to support the change.

■ Mis-starts – the change was badly implemented, its implementation had to be stopped and restarted, so it lost credibility.

■ The change process was delegated to outsiders (for example, consultants or contractors) who did not know the organisation sufficiently well to understand what would work and how.

■ The right people (those who would be affected by the change) were not consulted or were consulted too late.

■ The change might be valid at a strategic level, but little thought was given to its implementation or the need to tailor it, based on geography, culture or local need.

You will, doubtless, be able to add many more reasons for failure from your own experience. The sad fact is that we know how to make change work – we have known for eons! – but we are not always given the time, support, budget or freedom to make the changes work.

Here are some simple ideas to help you to implement your solutions:

■ *Involvement:* Involve those who will be affected by the change or have a political interest in it from the outset. Many of the problem-solving techniques described here can involve people at all levels without giving a bigger voice to the more senior/ vocal/political. Their involvement brings them in to the process and, effectively, denies them the right to change the outcomes because they were part of the group that agreed on how something should be done (and there will be many witnesses who saw them agreeing!)

- *Consultation:* Gather together at the outset anyone who may be affected by your proposed changes/solutions and use the force-field analysis to explore what may help/hinder the implementation of your solution. This way, those affected forfeit the right to say that they were not consulted. Of course, if you involve them in creating the solution at the outset, they have already forfeited this right!

- *Leadership buy-in:* Get leadership buy-in from the outset, either by involving them in the problem-solving process or working with them between crafting and implementing your solution.

- *Timing:* Pay attention to timing. People are tired of constant change. Wait until the time is right for your idea rather than being carried away on a tide of enthusiasm because it is high on your agenda.

- *Context:* Contextualise everything. When people understand why something is necessary, they are more likely, if not to support it, then at least to step out of the way to allow it to happen.

- *Talk to them as adults:* Do not patronise people. Often, in times of change, managers and leaders adopt a parental stance and treat their staff like stupid children. If you are having grown-up conversations all the time with your staff, change will not come as a surprise and, even when the results of the change may be difficult to accept, it is far easier to explain them if you have (and maintain) an adult relationship with your staff.

- *Translate strategy into practice:* Remember that strategic change has to be translated into practice. If you are relatively senior, you may be privy to strategic conversations in which your staff members take no part. Your staff suffer the fallout of your strategic deliberations without being part of the process and may not understand the reasons why certain decisions have been made. Explain them in purely practical terms. Pre-empt questions like, 'Can you help me to understand this?' and 'What does this mean in practice?'

- *Plan it:* Plan the implementation of your solution as rigorously as you can to avoid false starts and the resultant loss of credibility.

- *Play it down:* Remember that most of your staff will not be frightened of change, but indifferent to it. Do not make a big issue out of something that does not have a huge effect on your staff or colleagues. It is important to you, but may be of little consequence to them. Making a fuss of something is more likely to arouse strong emotions than being low key.

# What did you think of this book?

We're really keen to hear from you about this book, so that we can make our publishing even better.

Please log on to the following website and leave us your feedback.

It will only take a few minutes and your thoughts are invaluable to us.

www.pearsoned.co.uk/bookfeedback

# INDEX